"Something new and very [...] rowing literature: Peter Mall[...]
Pete has distilled a lifetim[...] competitor, coach, observer a[...] ...e, very interesting treatise on this obse[...] that continues to capture our hearts and minds.
Read on, and then go for a good, hard row."
- Brad Alan Lewis, Olympic Gold Medalist
and author of *Assault on Lake Casitas*

"Peter, you've been on a quest, and it happens to be a quest that we both share. I personally find your book enormously compelling, and the language you use has added depth and perspective to my own understanding of boat moving. Your descriptions are accurate, on track, and I admire what you've done.
I strongly recommend this book to *every* rower and coach."
- Steve Gladstone, University of California,
2000 U.S. Collegiate Champion Coach

"You know me. When in doubt, get a bigger hammer. But if you want to be smart and try to figure out how to use the hammer properly, take a look at Peter Mallory's *An Out-of-Boat Experience*. Wind your way through this book of discovery, and see if you agree with where Peter's journey has taken him.
Is he right? I don't know, but I'm going to have some fun working it out, and even if he's wrong, I'll learn something along the way.
Maybe this old dog can learn a new trick."
- Tiff Wood, 1983 World Bronze Medalist,
protagonist in *The Amateurs*
by David Halberstam

To David Katz —
I wrote this book
just for you. Let me
know what you think.

Enjoy

team_mallory@hotmail.com

AN
OUT-OF-BOAT
EXPERIENCE

... or
God is a Rower, and He Rows Like
Me!

by Peter Mallory

AN OUT-OF-BOAT EXPERIENCE
... or
God is a Rower, and He Rows Like *Me!*

Copyright 2000 *by Peter Mallory*

On the cover: the 1989 U.S. Masters Champion San Diego Rowing Club B Cox Four.
Back cover: Cox'n Kristin Bailey, Bow Peter Mallory, two man Rick Lopez
Front Cover: three man Glenn Schweighardt, stroke Tim Watenpaugh

Cover photo by SportGraphics. Now, seriously, can you even imagine a big regatta any more *without* the SportGraphics tent? How did our sport survive the 110 years between Thomas Eakins and SportGraphics?

It's a mystery to me!

ISBN: 1-885516-08-8

First Printing, October, 2000

San Diego Writers' Monthly Press
3910 Chapman Street
San Diego, California 92110-5694
USA
(619) 224-1050
team_mallory@hotmail.com

Introduction

"Whether I shall turn out to be the hero of my own life,
or whether that station will be held by anybody else,
these pages must show."
　　　　　　　　　　　　- *David Copperfield,* Charles Dickens

This book is one *very* opinionated man's journey in the sport of rowing, and that very opinionated man is *me!*

The stories contained within have been aching to get out for decades, but the urge has gotten ever stronger since I've entered the second 1,000 meters of my 2,000-meter life.

I feel a genetic imperative to pass on what I've learned while I still have breath in my body.

I write for my family.

I write for my son.

I write to exorcise my demons, set the record straight, settle a couple of scores, but also to pay tribute to those who have been my family for most of my life and who have helped to shape me. I write to pass on the joy and the wisdom that age has now afforded me.

I write for my family.

You are my family.

I write for you.

Rower or not, with or without calluses on your hands, it matters not. We are family, for you and I have experienced life . . . and life is a metaphor for rowing.

"Life is a metaphor for rowing."
　　　　　　　　　　　　- Peter Mallory

In this life, one way or another, my story is your story.

I write for you.

I write while I still have time. I write to complete the circle.

> *"When I am dead, I hope it may be said:*
> *'His sins were scarlet, but his book was read.'"*
> – with apologies to Hilaire Belloc

Incidentally, all of the stories contained in this book are absolutely true as I remember them. I have been accused of exaggeration in the past, but there has been no exaggeration this time around.
No need! Imagine that!

Eric Loberg and Billy Brown, I have treated our intertwined paths as a fable, and I have obtained your permission. As for the rest of you, I have been Joe Friday.

But to all of you I say:
"This is my personal reminiscence, so please don't confuse this book with history. Others have a perfect right to remember things their way, and I'm sure several will."

No. This is my journey. My odyssey. Mine alone.

And thanks so much to all my friends, rowers and civilians, who have read my manuscript and offered their support and perspective.
Special thanks to Mike MacCarthy of *San Diego Writers' Monthly*.

Peter Mallory
Del Mar, California
July 4, 2000

Prologue

On June 5, 1963, I graduated from Shortridge High School in Indianapolis, Indiana.

And so I am a Shortridge Blue Devil.

I am a Hoosier.

But by more than a generation I missed running into the most famous of my fellow Shortridge Blue Devils and fellow Hoosiers, the novelist Kurt Vonnegut.

He was that much older than I was.

After he graduated from Shortridge High School, Kurt Vonnegut attended Cornell University in Ithaca, New York. I, too, could have attended Cornell University. They accepted me, and I thought hard about it.

But still I would have missed running into Kurt Vonnegut.

To this day he remains that much older than I.

My loss. That I never met him . . . because I always felt that we had so much in common, the two of us being fellow Shortridge Blue Devils and fellow Hoosiers and all.

Over the ensuing years I've felt like he was a father figure of sorts to me.

Before I left Indianapolis, Indiana, before I began my competitive rowing and coaching career, I shopped often at Vonnegut's Hardware Store.

Best I could manage under the circumstances.

Is This a Small World or What?

On June 13, 1995, I climbed to the top of Half Dome in Yosemite National Park, to the top of the largest chunk of granite in the world, or so the guidebooks say, the last 900 vertical feet being negotiated hand-over-hand up a cable, by golly.

One of my best buddies from high school, a fellow Shortridge Blue Devil and fellow Hoosier, organized the hike for a group of his friends who were all reaching the half-century mark that year, myself included.

In celebration of a milestone in our lives.

> *"How many days . . .*
> *has it been since I was born?*
> *How many days . . .*
> *'til I die?"*
>
> - Leon Russell

Just for good luck, I wear my very last remaining University of Pennsylvania Lightweight Crew racing jersey, faded, decades old, just like I am.

On the way up the mountain, one of the other guys in the group strikes up a conversation with me. He's recognized my shirt. Seems, way back when, he rowed for Cornell University in Ithaca, New York.

I toss off a line, something like, "Isn't that interesting?"

But once I think for a moment, I realize I really *am* interested!

I mean we're both turning fifty, so we must have been in the same college class back then. I look at him, and he's lightweight size. In fact, fit as I might be, at that moment he's a lot closer to making weight than I am.

I ask him what boat did he row in?

"What boat did you row in?"

He says, "Second freshman lightweights."

I ask him, "What seat?"

He says, "Seven."

4

(Even after decades, how easy it is to slip back into the universal language of oarsmen. Back then there was no male or female, so collegiate rowers were first boat or second boat, freshman or varsity, heavyweight or lightweight, sitting somewhere between the "one" or bow seat and the "eight" or stroke seat, or else they were the cox'n, you know, the guy who steers.

That's it.

So this fellow walking beside me could tell me just about his whole rowing history in four words flat: "second" "freshman" "lightweight" "seven.")

But that's not the amazing part. The amazing part is that *I* rowed in the second freshman lightweight seven seat for my *own* college, for my beloved Penn Quakers, in our race *against* the Cornell Big Red!

Is this a small world or what?

On this trail in the middle of Yosemite National Park on a beautiful June morning beside a babbling brook, at the age of 49 years and 364 days, I have actually run into the very guy who beat me in my very first collegiate crew race, who had won from me my very first University of Pennsylvania Lightweight Crew racing jersey . . .

. . . and as I keep talking to him I realize he can hardly recall a single thing about how our paths first crossed thirty-one years earlier, on the day I began my rowing odyssey in his ancient Ithaca.

As for me, I remember every single detail of that cold and misty April day in 1964 on Cayuga's waters.

* * * * *

The Penn Lightweight Crew has come up from Philadelphia by bus. I am sporting a shaved head from Kappa Sigma Fraternity pledging, and this Saturday morning I have put on the venerated Pennsylvania racing jersey for the very first time. White t-shirt with two horizontal red stripes across my chest and a blue "P" with an oar through it over my heart, a heart that I can tell you is bursting with pride at this moment.

As the boats line up at the start along the Cayuga's western shore, the old and musty Cornell boathouse is far behind us up the inlet at the south end of the lake, with the campus looming high above. I look around and peer past my teammates. I can't quite make out the finish line a long mile and five-sixteenths away.

That's how far they row at the Royal Henley Regatta on the Thames River in England, or so I have been told.

The most famous regatta in the world. Cox'ns wear coats and ties, can you believe it? The Queen comes, or at least Prince Philip or Princess Anne or the Queen Mum, women in their finest frocks, men in blazers and boaters.

Every rower on Earth wants to row at Henley at least once in his lifetime, and me not the least.

"A mile and five." The fabled Henley distance. Soon I will be its master on Lake Cayuga!

Our opponents sit quietly beside us, and there's not a breath of wind. The lake is like a mirror. Deathly still. I can *hear* my heart beating.

"CORNELL, CORNELL, B. M. A."

Earlier in the morning, back at the boathouse I ran into Chris Williams, a classmate of mine from boarding school, now a Cornellian, and now stroking their first freshman lightweight boat.

Wow!

I am impressed. I never really got to know Chris during my days at Kent, our prep school, my father's prep school, perched on the banks of the mighty Housatonic River in northwestern Connecticut, where crew is life, and life is divided into port and starboard.

I never finished at Kent, left in the midst of my fifth form year, too soon to have seen Chris rise to stroke of the Kent JVs.

Rowers are Gods at Kent, the Greek Gods of Mt. Olympus. The Captain of the Crew is referred to, quite *seriously*, as "Zeus," and oarsmen stride the campus walks with all others receding around them.

In my absence Chris became a deity under the tutelage of Tote Walker, the ageless embodiment of what rowing stood for in all of our minds.

Tote was already a venerable institution at Kent when he coached my Dad in 1937. And Tote was still at it in the 1960s.

Go ahead. Do the arithmetic.

T. Dixon Walker was older than some of the stained glass windows in the Kent chapel.

Tote went to Heaven a few years ago. Grown men all around the world cried.

I never got to be coached by Tote Walker. I left too soon, but even if I'd stayed all the way to the end, I had been tiny, five feet tall and hardly more than 100 pounds, way too weenie to wear the hallowed and historied Blue and Gray, too weenie to wield an oar for Kent.

So, today, Chris is surprised to see me rowing at all. The last time he had seen me I was a cox'n in the intramural program at Kent . . . and a not very good one at that!

And now Chris is wearing White and "Cornellian" (whatever you do, don't call it *red!*), while I am decked in the traditional colors of the Penn.

> *"Hurrah . . . Hurrah . . . Hurrah . . . Hurrah . . .*
> *Hurrah for the Red and the Blue."*
> - University of Pennsylvania school song

Chris explains to me that B.M.A. stands for "Best Men Afloat." I am additionally impressed. Penn may have a marvelous school song, a couple of great songs in fact, but we cannot match the Cornell Crew cheer.

Funny thing about Cornell University. I told you I was accepted at Cornell. I intended to be an architect back then, so I applied to the three best architecture programs in the country: Yale, Cornell and Penn. Wait-listed at Yale, admitted to the other two.

Never liked Yale that much, to the consternation of my Yale-educated father, no particular reason I can tell you today, but probably *because* of my Yale-educated father.

Loved the other two colleges when I visited the campuses.

They were so different: Cornell an undergraduate architecture program, Penn in graduate school, Cornell rural, Penn urban, on and on, back and forth.

I couldn't decide.

Finally, it occurred to me.

I was a shrimp! Kids kicked sand in my face, stole my lunch money. All my life I had been picked last on the playground. I will be lucky to get up to 120 pounds with rocks in my pockets by the time of my high school graduation!

No way I could make the lightweight crew at Cornell. Lightweights didn't look like *me!* They were tall strong 150 pounders, not short scrawny 120 pounders, and Cornellians weren't just lightweights. They were the absolute best lightweights in the country!

The *best!*

And so I chose Penn . . . under the assumption they were crappy enough that I actually might have a chance to make the squad!

And a great choice it turned out to be, stupendous choice in fact . . . but what a horrendous thought process!

Imagine my shame!

Imagine my good fortune!

But all that decision-making has been forgotten a year later as I fidget at the start line in Ithaca. Awaiting the commands from the officials I am supremely confident, conveniently ignoring not only Cornell's continuing supremacy in collegiate lightweight rowing but also the fact that my Penn boat has yet to execute more than thirty strokes in a row at race pace, even in practice!

. . . ignoring the fact that I am the only member of my crew to have even sat in a boat before six months ago, and that as a cox'n.

But what the Hell do I know?

I don't tell Chris Williams this, but I was still a cox'n just a month ago, when my body finally decided to start filling out. And now, instead of steering and sitting right *in front* of the eight man, the "stroke" man, the man who sets the pace for all the rest of us, I am manning the oar right *behind* him. I can even whisper in his ear . . . that is, if I were the whispering type.

I am the backbone of the crew. I am the *seven* man!

A MAN, no longer a boy, come of age this very day, the hand of Odysseus resting comfortably on my shoulder, the strength of Hercules coursing through my body.

The officials line up the two boats. I feel something warm. I look down. There is a wet spot slowly spreading from the center of my shorts.

"Are you ready? . . . *Row!*"

Our stroke man is Bill Fogler, from Toronto, Ontario, who eats fast and diets hard. He didn't eat for a week to make weight, and back at the dock I noticed his eyes still had that crazed look of a religious zealot.

"Fogie" takes us off the line at 44 strokes per minute. Now normally we can't even count that high, let alone row that high, but in our god-like state, it feels just fine.

I sneak a look over to the other boat. I am still even with my counterpart, the Cornell seven man. We haven't yet taken the lead.

Hmm! I guess our worthy opponents are actually going to make us earn this fine first win of the year, this first win of our college careers!

Jimmy Beggs, Penn's freshman coach, hasn't made the trip. He is with the freshman heavies, so we lightweights are on our own. Other observers in the launch remark that Cornell has settled to a sensible and conservative 29 strokes per minute, Penn to a seldom-seen 41.

"Fascinating contrast of styles," they muse.

"Isn't there a story," one remarks, "a story about a Japanese crew that once rowed a whole race at 40 . . . and didn't they all die of heart attacks or something?"

(A rowing urban legend, one of many, I am destined to find out later.)

"Perhaps these young Penn fellows will get a lesson in history today." The group murmurs its agreement as the boats make their way down the course.

Back within our boat we are oblivious as we fast approach the Anaerobia County line. The next time I look over, I am even with the stroke man, and so we are now a seat behind. A bit later it's two. Cornell seems to be just inching away.

Hmm!

Everything is happening . . . in . . . slow . . . motion . . .

Hey! Is that pain in my lungs? I can't describe it. I don't want to describe it! Are we even halfway done yet?

Now I have to turn my head further and further to even catch a glimpse of the Cornell rudder . . .

What's that?   Could the stroke rate be faltering?

"Keep it up, Fogie!" I exclaim supportively. "Keep it up, Fogie!"

I look over at shore as we crawl by cozy cottages.   Now, when I turn my head, I have forgotten all about the other boat.   All I care about is the finish line.   "A mile and five."   Where the *HELL* is it?

* * * * *

It is Monday, two days later.   After class, as we head for practice, my lungs still ache.   Two whole days later!   Imagine that!

Coach Beggs asks us how the race went.   The bow man bursts out,

"We lost by five lengths!   We must have rowed the entire race at 40 with Pete yelling all the way, 'TAKE IT UP, FOGIE!   TAKE IT UP, FOGIE!'"

Turned to Dust

Gentleman Jim Beggs, one of the two men in my lifetime to coach regularly in a three-piece suit, nods thoughtfully . . . and switches me *way* back in the boat, where presumably I can give Fogie no more bad advice.

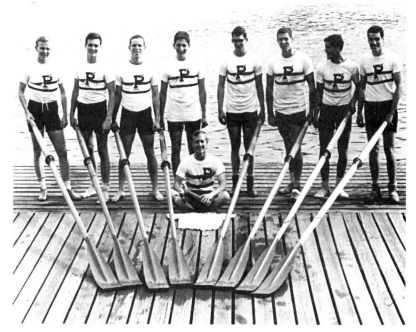

photo credit: the Mallory Collection

That's Bill Fogler, our stroke man, on the far right.
That's me, head shaved, third from the left, where Coach Beggs switched me.

* * * * *

And now three decades have passed, and I am hiking beside a guy who has almost forgotten our day together on Lake Cayuga.

All collegiate crew races end in a shirt bet, winner take all, and the shirt he won from me that day has long ago turned to dust.

11

And, get this, he never rowed again after his freshman year. Had his fill. Left the family of oarsmen, concentrated on his studies. Kicked my ass and moved on.

Isn't life grand?

As for me, I keep going . . . through college . . . after college . . . through decades of rowing and coaching and rowing again . . . still at it.

Here I am writing about it.

And I'm rowing with my son, a fourth generation rower.

No Problemo

August 20, 1989. Lake Merritt, downtown Oakland on a lovely, sunny California day. It's 500 meters to go in the semi-finals of the U.S. Masters National Rowing Championships.

I am racing in the San Diego Rowing Club entry in the Men's B Cox Four, for crews 35-years-of-age and older, and we are open water ahead of the field, cruising along at maybe half pressure.

(That's us on the cover of this book!)

From my lofty position in the bow seat I am surveying the race as it unfolds behind us, and I am very, very pleased with myself. At 5'10" with 184 pounds honed by more than a decade of coaching from a single shell and a solid year of weight lifting and hill running, at the age of 44 I am the fittest I have ever been in my entire life.

Oh yes!

And I am closing in on my life long quest for the Holy Grail.

Oh yes!

After fifty national championships as a coach, I am finally in position to win my *first* as an oarsman.

And it has been a very, very long time coming . . .

And look who I'm rowing with!

Look at my family!

My stroke is Tim Watenpaugh, 6'4", 210 pounds, and club captain. I coached him many years earlier at San Diego State before he went on to Penn A.C. in Philadelphia and to the 1979 U.S. Pan American Team.

In the three seat is Glenn Schweighardt, president of our esteemed club, 6'2" 195. Fifteen years ago I was coach of the inaugural Mission Bay Rowing Association crew when Glenn won the first two of his basket-full of national medals.

No, seriously, he really keeps them in a basket!

These two guys are the heart of the boat, and, truth be told, Glenn and Tim *both* wanted to be the stroke man this summer.

Now each guy in a four has a single oar. In order to make the boat go straight, obviously two guys have to have their oars on the port side of the boat and two guys on starboard.

At San Diego Rowing Club all the serious rowers can row with one oar, called "sweep rowing," which we're doing now, and they can also row with two oars, called "sculling."

And most can wield their sweep oar on either side, on port or on starboard. I can. Glenn can.

Tim can . . . but he doesn't. He has a tricky back, and he tries not to throw his body any unnecessary metaphorical curve balls. He stays on starboard.

And so to balance off Tim, Glenn's rowing on port in our four.

The sport of rowing is loaded down with tradition, and boats are traditionally built so the stroke man has to row on port. The metal outrigger at his seat is simply bolted to the boat on that particular side.

But our shell is a magical stripped-down zebra-striped carbon-fiber beauty, custom made for us by the Keebler elves at Kaschper Racing Shells in Lucan, Ontario.

Get this! Our shell can be rerigged to starboard stroke!

Well, the last few months we'd show up to the boathouse, and it seemed our boat was different every week, and either Glenn or Tim would be stroking it, depending on whether Glenn or Tim had last touched it.

It was really funny.

And about the closest we could get to a conflict in this wonderful boat.

Made no difference to me, port stroke or starboard, Glenn or Tim. I took my seat in bow, thanked God for my good fortune, and rowed whatever side I had a rigger on.

Finally, it came down to me, as everybody's former coach, to tell Glenn that the boat seemed go just a scooch better with Tim stroking this year. And so, finally just a few weeks ago, Glenn settled into the three seat, and the boat stopped being rerigged every few days.

In the two seat is Rick Lopez, 6'2" 190, Naval Academy grad, slow talker. I had taught him to scull while he was a Naval officer stationed in San Diego during the 70s. Now he's a copilot for Delta Airlines, a multiple national champion . . . and he likes the port side.

14

(Navy guys seem to prefer consistency.)

No problemo.

"All my life I have been preparing to row in this boat. Port? Starboard? I'll take whatever's left . . . And starboard it is!"

So says Peter Mallory.

You know, I had even coached our cox'n, Kristin Bailey. To maintain a low center of gravity, she's lying down and steering from the skinny section of the shell between my bow seat and the bow ball.

(If you look carefully, you can see her on the back cover. Yes, that's the back of her head.)

And Kristin isn't just a passenger, isn't just along for the ride, nossirree. Cox'ns have a lot of responsibility besides steering. They are the brains of the boat.

And Kristin has *experience!* She's been a champion junior rower for me, so she knows both sides of the sport, and when she says something, we trust and respect her judgment. Oh yes.

Yes. Look at my boat!

"We are Fa-mi-ly!"
- the Pointer Sisters

In years and decades past I had sown these dragon's teeth, and now I am harvesting the fruits of a lifetime of coaching effort.

I am Argos, the architect and the ancient mariner of our boat.

It's a fine crew: strong, competent, fit, experienced, a genuine joy to row in, and how often can you say that of a boat? I'm so proud . . . and so honored to be invited to be a part of it.

My mind wanders, as it does so often in my life.

My mind wanders to the race arrayed behind us. Our opponents' colorful jerseys, their painted oars glinting in the sunlight. The other five boats on the course with us are all neck and neck, straining to be among the remaining two semi-final qualifiers for tomorrow's six-boat final. It's a great race, and I have a great seat from which to watch it.

Somebody's cox'n over to the left somewhere attempts to spur on his crew by telling them San Diego might be tiring.

"Pour it on, guys! I think San Diego might be tiring!"

15

San Diego?

Us?

> *"You don't frighten us, English pig dogs! Go and*
> *boil your bottoms, sons of a silly person!"*
> — Monty Python and the Holy Grail

But silently I give the cox'n permission to fib a little if he thinks it will help his team.

For he is entertaining me.

I float overhead. I observe myself and my teammates from above . .

And I'm having an out-of-boat experience . . .

. . . unstuck in time, and I've been here before . . .

. . . *déjà vu*. . .

. . . in this very situation . . . in 1965, in fact.

How many years ago is that now? Twenty four?

I can see it, smell it even, the very first of my oh-so-many trips to the U.S. Nationals.

Mallory! Will You Shut the Fug Up?

Nineteen sixty-five has been pretty special for me. I finished my second year at Penn rowing in the six seat of the lightweight varsity, quite a step up from my humble beginnings during freshman year.

For our post-sophomore summer, most of us have migrated a couple of doors up Boathouse Row to the esteemed Undine Barge Club, following our coach, Fred Leonard, who has just completed his inaugural year at the helm of the Penn Lightweights.

Fred had done his rowing at Undine . . . and Cornell.

(Cornell again. Hmm!

And if you ever owned a boat, you probably already know Fred Leonard. Chances are he's your insurance man!

Is this a small world or what?)

"Esteemed Undine Barge Club?" More like shifting foundations, peeling paint, sagging docks. A jewel of a boathouse designed by Frank Furness, Philadelphia's gift to 19th-century American architecture, a jewel of a boathouse now tarnished and falling into disrepair. Filled mostly with old boats and old farts in blue blazers telling us stories about how they had rowed "that very boat over there on that rack" to some national medal or other back in the 20s, and we were darned lucky to still have it around for a new generation to row.

"Yeah, right!" we would reply . . . under our breath.

Philadelphia. No place in the world quite like it.

> *"I'd rather be in Philadelphia."*
> - epitaph of W.C. Fields

Boathouse Row. The Schuylkill Navy!

Philadelphia Girls Club, Undine, Penn A.C., University of Pennsylvania, Vesper, Malta, University Barge, on and on, all in a line. Rivalries that went back a century and more. Families torn asunder when a son changed clubs. Reminds me of Gettysburg, 150 miles to the West.

I was quickly taught that most Catholics rowed for Penn A.C. (Not true!) and there was no intelligent life downstream of Bachelors Barge (The jury's still out on that one.).

Undine and Vesper both have summer lightweight crews this year. Lightweights actually weigh in before a race. Average 150 pounds per man.

There are no official height restrictions in rowing, but it helps your leverage to be tall, and the best lightweights are over six feet. Not me. At 5'10" I have to make up for my shortcomings with orneriness.

Which I do. Oh my, yes!

Vesper's boathouse is right next to Penn. We even share a dock, and we don't dislike them or anything, but when our lightweights race their lightweights there's a lot of yelling back and forth.

Of course I'm in the thick of it.

"Hey Geoff! That's quite a sunburn you have. Got it at the Jersey Shore yesterday, did you? Are you sure you should be out here rowing today?

"Oh, I see you're not pulling very hard. Very wise! I'm sure your teammates will be happy to pull a bit harder to make up for . . ."

"Mallory! Will you shut the *fug* up?!"

That very well reasoned and appropriate response inevitably comes from the Vesper cox'n, John Hartigan, a fellow Quaker, but already years past graduation at Penn, an attorney who wears business suits and has a family and everything! A real adult. A grown-up.

I am fascinated by his *shoes*. They're wing tips, just like my Dad's, and always perfectly shined.

Just like my Dad's.

John Hartigan seems incredibly old to the lost boys of Undine, and I got such a hoot hearing an adult cuss me out.

I never got to row in a boat coxed by John Hartigan. Not even once. My loss. He's a world champion now. Even back then he was that good, and he knew every trick in the book . . . except how to shut me the you-know-what up.

"Sorry John! I see you have your hands full. But keep an eye on Palsy in the six seat, John. He's rushing his slide."

18

"Malloryyyyy . . . "

All this during every local match race. Middle of the race. We never let up, as we are much faster than Vesper's lightweights. We toy with them, taunt them, pull their wings off one by one.

Sweet.

Juvenile, in retrospect, I must admit. Shame on me . . .

* * * * *

I can report today that in the thirty-five years that have now transpired since the summer of 1965, John Hartigan has not spoken a single word to me, despite the fact that we are fellow Quakers and all. He has pretended I am invisible and unhearable, on the water and off.

And he paid me back seven years later . . . yes indeed!

* * * * *

By the time 1972 comes around, I am coaching in the afternoon, and so I have to train in the mornings in my single, in my brand new *Stämpfli* single, my pride and joy, the best boat made anywhere in the world, the *Ferrari* of racing shells, just off the plane from Switzerland.

It's darn lonely rowing on the Schuylkill River in the mornings, but one of my best friends, Robby Meek, is also training this year.

Robby is tall and lanky, a sweet man on a Harley Davidson. We are fellow Hoosiers, in fact both from the same neighborhood in Indianapolis, Indiana. Our parents have been friends for years. Is this a small world or what!

But Robby and I only met as undergraduates at Penn.

As an oarsman, Robby's *good!* He won the Pan American pairs title in 1967 with another fellow Quaker with the remarkable name of Gardner Cadwalader.

For the Olympic year of 1972 Robby has teamed up with a new partner named Guy Iverson, from the Midwest somewhere, tall as Robby, strong as an ox, formidable reputation, National Team experience.

And John Hartigan is their cox'n.

This seems a perfect combination. America's very best, together in a cox pair.

They are the *talk* of Boathouse Row!

Robby and I chat one day. Every morning we are just about the only two boats on the river. They have no other pair to row with, and I have no other single. And a good lightweight single (like me!) is about as fast as a good heavyweight cox pair (like them!).
We conclude it makes perfect sense to practice together.
"Let's practice together, Pete!"
"That's a *great* idea, Robby!"

The next day we arrive together at Boathouse Row. John objects to our plans for shared workouts, but only to Robby.
(I'm invisible, remember?)
I offer to just row along, row hard, stay quiet. I promise quiet. I promise to behave myself. John can run everything. I'll just follow. *I promise!*
Robby says "Yes!"
John says "No!"
Guy says nothing. (He wasn't much of a talker back then, reminded me of a taciturn northern Minnesota Norwegian farmer.
I wonder why.)
Robby's embarrassed, says it's a free country, tells me to come on along and see how it goes.
"Come on along, Pete! It's a free country. Let's see how it goes," says my friend and fellow Quaker and fellow Indianapolitan and fellow Hoosier.

John looks pissed.

We're out together this one morning a few days later, and I figure the pair must be doing intervals of some sort. They would suddenly accelerate with no warning, row like Hell for some period of time, and then ease off to a paddle, again with no warning.
I'm next to them . . . and clueless.
John seems to be calling the workout as quietly as possible so I can't hear his commands, but I'm doing okay. I don't complain.

I am energized. At least I have some company for a change. Robby and I exchange pleasantries between the hard pieces. John never looks my way.

It's a great workout for me. Our two boats are competitive, and I am rowing my ass off to prove myself to Robby . . . and to John.

I row alongside the pair, steering off its wake, following the disturbances left as their starboard oar exits the water at the end of each stroke. Each disturbance or "puddle" is a tiny whirlpool in the muddy surface of the Schuylkill River.

I never look all the way around to see where I am going. I only occasionally glance to my side to ensure I am just outside the pair's puddles. It's uncomfortable for me to actually place my own oar within the little whirlpools, so I lurk just outside, hoping never to be sucked in.

We are heading home now, two more straight-aways before we get back to the boathouse. I am at my redline, *definitely* not looking around now, putting everything into every stroke, relying on memory to tell me where I am on the river.

We are in the middle of a hard piece. We have been rowing maybe two minutes, and, as usual, I have no idea how long it's going to last before John will have the other boat ease off and prepare for the next effort. I am keying off the pair. They are just inches off the tip of my port oar and maybe six feet ahead of me and . . .

BANG!

I've hit the bridge. Just a glancing blow on the rigger, thank Heavens. My brand new *Stämpfli* single, my pride and joy, the best boat made anywhere in the world, the *Ferrari* of racing shells, just off the plane from Switzerland!

Into the bridge. The railroad bridge. Sinister stone monolith. Scylla to John Hartigan's Charybdis.

I am stunned. Astonished. My life stops . . .

The pair has kept going.
Robby calls from far ahead to see if I'm okay?
"Are you okay, Pete?"
I'm not sure, but I nod and wave anyway.

I start to look around. Where the Hell am I?

Hmm!

John Hartigan, the most skillful cox'n I have ever met, a man who can thread a needle in a boat, has steered clear across the river, completely against the traffic pattern.

Son of a bitch!
He knew I was following him, steering off him, and he ran a pick on that bridge abutment, just like we were playing basketball.
Son of a bitch!

He steered me straight into that bridge! Must have assumed I would stop. Never counted on me not looking around. Never counted on me actually *trusting* him not to endanger me or my boat.

Thank Heavens *Stämpfli* makes such sturdy shells. My beautiful wooden boat has survived and will reappear in this book.

Needless to say, we never practice together again, my lightweight single and their heavyweight cox pair, so competitive, one to another.

* * * * *

But, listen to this! That pair turns out to be a prime example of one of the greatest mysteries in the sport of rowing . . . a mystery that haunted me for decades and has become the central issue of this book.
We didn't know it at the time, but it turned out I wasn't going all that fast that spring in my single, and, as for the pair, they totally reeked!
No wonder John didn't want anybody around.
Iverson/Meek/Hartigan turned out to be dreadfully slow. Truly awful. All that potential on paper . . . and *trente-six fois merde* slow on the water!

How could that be?
Good question.

Incidentally, I figure John Hartigan and I are even now. And I still like his shoes.

Only Two Places in a Race

Meanwhile, back to 1965. Back to our story.

Vesper's heavyweights won the Olympics in the eight in 1964, so every stud in the country is trying out for their first boat in 1965. We lightweights at Undine spend the entire summer doing 500 after 500-meter piece of interval training, against not the Vesper lightweights, but against the Vesper second heavyweight eight.

Wow!

We lose by a seat, win by a seat, back and forth, rowing at 40 strokes per minute the whole way, times around 1:25 . . . about as fast as a good man can run . . . darn fast for anybody in a boat back then . . . *flying for lightweights!*

Every day there's a rumor, and we half hope the Vesper *first* eight will show up!

We have a simply wonderful Undine lightweight eight.

For example, years earlier, our stern pair, Manno and Walsh, LaSalle College High School, won the Philadelphia Scholastic Quadruple Sculls Championship . . . in a *double!* The two of them against lots of boats with four scullers each.

(Rowing urban legend number two . . . except this one is true!)

And we have old guys, guys who have rowed for years and years. Not as old as John Hartigan, perhaps, but nevertheless guys who shave every day!

Unlike me. I am the baby of the boat, twenty years old, and have rowed seriously for just over a year!

All summer before the Nationals we compete in doubles and singles, but we never actually get to enter our eight in a big race, a race that actually counts. Can't go to the Canadian Henley, that greatest of spectacles on the North American continent. Somebody has an actual grown-up excuse, a job conflict or something.

So it all comes down to the U.S. Nationals on Hunter Island Lagoon at Orchard Beach in the borough of the Bronx, not fifteen miles from the Empire State Building in Manhattan. You can just make it out in the distance on a clear day.

Final only. Six boats. One shot at immortality.

Our debut.

* * * * *

Now Orchard Beach had hosted the U.S. Olympic Rowing Trials just a year before in '64, and a special buoy system, first of its kind in the Western Hemisphere, was still installed on the course.

It had been only been a few years since the Albano Buoy System, was first introduced at the 1960 Olympics, and just like on Lago Albano outside Rome, the six lanes of the Hunter Island Lagoon course were separated from one another by rows and rows of buoys, spaced out every few meters.

Back then, each buoy was a primitive, cumbersome affair anchored by a cable to the bottom of the lagoon, heavily weighted and sporting a snappy triangular orange pennant atop an eighteen-inch wooden dowel. Made for quite a spectacle, I must say, as the breezes swept across the course from nearby Long Island Sound.

* * * * *

It's a lovely August dawn, not a cloud in the sky, as we strip to our skivvies to weigh in under the trees, surrounded by upturned boats, waiting on slings for their oarsmen to carry them down to the dock later in the day. Dr. Jack Sack, the tallest in our boat at six feet and more, how much more I cannot tell from my vantage point several inches below, Jack looks especially skinny in his sleeveless t-shirt. The sun has never touched his shoulders, and this is the first time he has actually made weight all summer. Saul Berman, our cox'n, is sporting a railroad engineer's hat. He doesn't have to weigh in like the rest of us, but he has been dieting nonetheless, doing his part. Billy Mastalski is actually tan under his shirt. He had done most of his rowing at Malta but came to Undine to row for our Fred.

A turncoat. A Johnny Reb.

After years in group showers, most of us are quite comfortable with our nudity, but my roommate for the summer, Milt Rossman, remains embarrassed to be nearly naked out here in the open. Don Callahan, coached by Fred when he was at Haverford School and now rowing for Trinity College, is joking to mask his relief at having made weight, and

Bill Wark, our bow man, is quiet as always, wearing glasses that make him look studious and thoughtful. For our stern pair, Manno and Walsh, this is old hat as they wolf down bread and honey after the whole boat has been stamped and certified lightweight.

I am nervous, keyed up. I have been preparing for this day for a whole year. It had seemed an eternity, and now it's unfolding before me with increasing alacrity.

I am sliding down the rabbit hole.

This afternoon as we row to the line, I feel like puking. I settle for peeing in my pants, now a Mallory tradition.

We have been assigned one of the middle lanes. From the starting line you can scan down your lane, and it looks like a bowling alley with flags . . . all the way to a point on the horizon.

Are you ready? . . . *Row!*

Two boats to our right, three to our left, "volleyed and thundered."

In twenty strokes we are open water ahead. Just like that . . .

Oh my! All the nervousness washes away in an instant. I am in the two seat and can see everything.

After our start we settle to a low 35 strokes per minute. After all those 500s, this is the lowest we have ever rowed this boat.

Everything . . . is . . . in . . . slow . . . motion.

Our opponents' colorful jerseys, their painted oars glinting in the sunlight. How bright they are! How they scramble! I listen with amusement to all the cox'ns. They have come from all over the U.S. and Canada just to entertain me.

I float overhead. I observe myself and my teammates from far above

My first-ever out-of-boat experience . . .

At 1,000 meters we have at least three lengths. Just as it will again in 1989, my mind is wandering as my senses take everything in. I am very, very pleased with myself.

As I survey the course, the flags on the buoys are snapping smartly to the left. It is mid-afternoon, and there is a pleasant but persistent onshore breeze from the Sound, but I am thinking forward to my gold medal. On it is a crude bas-relief rendering of a 30-year-old professional oarsman named John Biglen, an 1874 based on work by Thomas Eakins, the famous painter and amateur sculler from Phila-delphia who knew Biglen well.

Now I feel a great deal of fondness for the works of Thomas Eakins. He's one of my absolute favorite artists, but there's no spon-taneity in his oeuvre, don't you agree? Even in his rowing pictures.

Insects caught in amber . . . that's what they are.

His paintings . . . everything planned and executed in his studio down on North Broad Street near the Pennsylvania Academy.

The meticulous perspective drawing for the Biglen portrait is now part of the collection at the Museum of Fine Arts in Boston. Note the reflections on the individual wavelets.

The watercolor study, my own personal favorite, more free and expressive, is at the Metropolitan in New York, while the finished oil painting is something of a disappointment by comparison, don't you think? The life of the watercolor is dissipated, ossified.

Yes, the oil painting's at Yale, and not really worth a separate trip to New Haven.

No. "John Biglen in a Single Scull" leaves something to be desired.

(Can you tell I'm an Art History major back at Penn?)

My reverie continues as I float above my boat as it courses down its lane of buoys on Hunter Island Lagoon.

I can feel the heft of the medal in my hand, the texture. An alloy of some sort, rather cheap, light, coated with a gold frosting of some sort, with a little circular ring at the top for the ribbon to be attached.

Rather pedestrian for something of such symbolic and emotional value!

The ribbon is red, white and blue. What else?

I will get the medal framed atop a photo of the boat, my national champion boat. I carefully select the place I will hang it in my living room, I imagine taking the subway surface car to Center City Philadelphia and walking up Walnut Street to the framing store. I select the mat material, perhaps a creamy parchment color to highlight the wood finish of our oars.

Ouch! Look at the estimate! $35.00? This is going to be expensive . . . but it's well worth it, don't you think?

I remind myself we will have to actually pose for that photo of the boat when we get back to shore, probably under the trees with the late afternoon sun streaming through the branches and the boat and the water in the background, oars up . . . no, oars down in front of us. Arrange them carefully. Make sure the photographer doesn't chop off the blades.

Can't ever trust the photographer, you know.

"Everybody smile! One more, just to be sure. Good! Congratulations, everybody! I'll make copies."

I'm thinking to myself: Peter Mallory, gold medalist, United States champion! Dammit, life is good! I am already taking off my shoes, standing on the couch, hammering the nail into the wall . . .

Now in my life up until this moment, halfway down the course in the Bronx, NY, on a sunny August day in 1965, I have actually coxed longer than I have rowed, coxed at Kent and then at Penn. Hell, I have coxed longer than our cox'n, longer even than Saul!

"Strangely believe it!"
- Mad Magazine

The cox'n inside of me notices that the wind has pushed us a bit sideways during my reverie. Our starboard oars are kind of close, soon *perilously* close to the buoys . . . and Saul isn't correcting.

Is his mind wandering? Is he, too, having an out-of-boat experience?

He's my good friend. We will be roommates in another year. Should I call out a warning to him?

But all summer we have been a team of chiefs and no Indians, everyone with an opinion, me worst of all, and all summer we have struggled to keep the talking in the boat to a minimum, at least when we weren't racing John Hartigan. I reluctantly keep my mouth shut and hope for the best.

Closer and closer we come.

Finally it happens. All four starboard oars, one by one, each in its turn, strike hard on one of the infernal, immovable buoys -- bang, Bang, BANG, <u>BANG</u>!

The boat shudders to a complete halt. We are in total shock. Our rhythm, our reveries have been blasted to pieces. We start again, but our composure has been shattered, and the field is already nipping at our heels.

Detroit gets by. Can we rally?

In the final 500 meters, I'm getting used to a new idea. I'm thinking to myself: Peter Mallory, silver medalist, United States runner-up.

* * * * *

Didn't work. We never did get around to taking a picture of that almost-marvelous boat.

Bridesmaids.

For us there were only two places in that race: first and shitty.

And so on that day I swore to myself I would embark upon a quest, a journey, I would row at least one more summer, one more Nationals, and earn the gold medal that had slipped from my grasp in that steady crosswind.

I wonder what I would have thought back then had I known how long I would eventually have to travel on that journey, how many continents I would cross, how many labors I would have to perform.

That Detroit boat? Stroked by Jim Dreher. Solid man. Go buy a boat or some oars from him. He and his wife Colleen run Durham Boat Company.

Is this a small world or what?

The Curse of the JV Scar

My Heavens, we were fast, that Undine lightweight eight of ours.

None faster in 1965. That day at Orchard Beach we were the best that we could be, the best in the country, in all of North America, in fact, and yet we didn't win.

In the ensuing years - no, the ensuing decades - I was to discover it's not that easy to be the best that you can be in a boat, especially at the precise moment when it's important.

But, oh my, it's even harder to cross the finish line first in this fickle sport that we practice. *So often* the best don't cross the finish line first.

Nevertheless, 1966 has been sweet. Lightweight varsity stroke.

photo credit: the Mallory Collection

1966 University of Pennsylvania Lightweight Varsity: Bow John Cantrill, O Captain! my Captain! Larry Walsh, Milt Rossman, Paul Garnerberg, cox'n Bob Nichol, Bob Harrison, Geoff Farmer, Martin Dominguez, stroke Peter Mallory.

But life is made up of peaks and valleys. Oh my, yes!

I came crashing down into a deep valley one late winter afternoon in 1967, my senior year at Penn.

A year of rowing for Fred Leonard has a certain rhythm to it. Starting in September and for most of the year, the Penn Lightweights row in even boats, Fred not tipping us off as to how we stand on the team.

One exception would be the Head of the Charles in October. My senior year, Fred boats a superbly experienced varsity eight with me in the stroke seat, and we win the open lightweight eight event at the Head by ten seconds, beating Harvard for what turns out to be the only time in my rowing career, and, in the process, setting a course record that will stand for a full decade.

Bravo Penn!

But then it's back to even boats until February, even March. Finally, the afternoon comes when we arrive at the boathouse and the lineups on the bulletin board are obviously Fred's first attempt at boating a varsity, junior varsity and third varsity crew for the spring racing season.

When that day finally comes in 1967, I can tell you I am much relieved to read that I will again be stroking the first boat, just as I did the previous fall on the Charles, and just as I did the entire previous spring.

And so I will complete my collegiate career at the top of my game on an increasingly competitive team, a team that I have helped improve from last in the East my freshman year to just maybe the best in the East by the time I graduate. I will earn my third varsity letter and, along with it, a coveted Penn Varsity Blanket.

Life is good.

Now most college coaches I have known in my life tend to dread that day each year when they first attempt to boat their varsity, for much of the time their preconceptions turn out to be disastrously off base. The second boat goes out and promptly thrashes the newly anointed first boat.

It happens over and over. Not just at Penn. All over.

Put the "best" guys in a boat, and, all too often, the boat is butt-slow. Remember Meek/Iverson/Hartigan?

Why does this happen? Nobody seemed to know exactly.

If you're a rower, it's probably happened to you, too. More than once, hasn't it? I bet you're smiling (or wincing) right now.

But you don't have to be a rower to relate. Contrary to conventional wisdom, it seems that all too often the shortest path in life is *not* the straight line.

The story always continues . . .

The coach goes back to the drawing board, makes change after change, seemingly at random, looking for some magic combination, everyone on pins and needles, everyone feeling like they are being judged on some ephemeral karma, rather than on something real and tangible like competence or fitness or strength or experience or courage.

Terrible feeling. Terrible situation. In many of these stories the coach never finds the solution.

How about you? Are you thinking of a story of your own right now?

I tell you, this story has been repeated countless times. The ultimate version that I've heard comes from Dartmouth in 1964 or '65, where the varsity heavyweight men continue to have trouble beating the JV in practice all the way up to the end of the spring. In frustration, the coach (must have been Pete Gardner, I suppose) schedules a do-or-die end-of-season race-off between the two boats . . . and the JV wins.

Of course.

So the first boat becomes the second boat and vice versa, and the boat that used to be the varsity and has all the "best" guys in it goes to the end-of-season IRA Regatta as the JV . . . and wins the JV national championship by open water.

As I recall, the Penn JVs end up second that year, and you can just imagine how pissed *they* were!

(I wonder if this Dartmouth story is another urban legend.)

I've heard lots of explanations for this JV vs. varsity phenomenon.

The guys relegated to the JV have something to prove . . . *so it's psychology.*

There is some indefinable quality that goes into a successful eight. You can't just put the best guys in a boat and expect it to go well . . . *so it's chemistry.*

My coach Fred Leonard used to talk about "boat moving."

A year earlier, I remember the two of us watching a very special Penn Heavyweight Freshman Crew win their first race of the season. These were absolutely enormous guys, nobody under 6'4", nobody under 195 pounds, and their stroke man was a quiet giant named Dexter Bell.

"Boy, that guy sure is a boat mover. He sure can move a boat," Fred said over and over as they rowed by with an enormous lead.

I looked . . . and I could tell he was big, and he certainly was rowing, but that's all I saw. Everybody else in the boat was big and rowing, too.

I asked Fred what he meant, what he saw that was so special about Dexter Bell in particular. He kept watching and mumbling something about how some people could just move boats, and Dexter Bell was just one of those people.

It seemed to be an axiom on Boathouse Row. Apparently, some people could and some people just couldn't "move boats." The funny thing was that Fred never once attempted to describe to us *how* to move boats. In fact, I never heard any coach describe it. It just seemed to be an accepted fact that you were either born with the gift or you weren't. It was part of your genetic heritage.

On that day in 1967 when I read on the bulletin board that I will stroke the Penn Lightweight Varsity for one more year, my varsity mates and I, all of us the "best" guys on the squad, manage to avoid the ignominy of losing to our own JV . . . but, unfortunately for us and for our peace of mind, the JV isn't all that far behind us at the end of the day.

Not a good sign.

As you would expect, weeks go by, Fred trying one change after another, trying to speed us up, looking for the right chemistry, but to no avail. We just aren't moving boats the way he knows we should.

Every day Fred scratches his head

* * * * *

Well, you know where this story is going. It's going to turn out that Peter Mallory's the problem, that *I'm* the one not moving boats, but the way it all unfolded . . .

* * * * *

I wake up from an unscheduled nap one afternoon and break into a cold sweat as I glance at the clock and realize I'm going to be late for practice. I jump in my car, race like a demon through the streets of West Philadelphia, leap out, run through the boathouse and out to the dock . . . just in time to see my team disappearing around the bend past the statue of Viking explorer Thorfinn Karlsefni at the end of Boathouse Row.

In my entire four years of college, I've never missed a single practice! This will be the only practice I am even late for. The *only* one!

Imagine that!

I stand on the dock, listening to the water gurgling under my feet, glancing at the cars across the river on the Schuylkill Expressway, looking down and staring at my leg curiously, as . . . if . . . it . . . belonged . . . to . . . someone . . . else.

Hmm!

The muscles of the right thigh are fully exposed through a deep gash, a window, if you will, a window into the interior of my leg. Fully developed quadriceps lateralis. Well defined. The product of three years of power squats. Excellent! Look at the individual fibers. Interesting.

Fascinating even . . .

Hmm!

Hmm!

What's wrong with this picture?

It takes me a minute or more to conclude that I must have run into a protruding metal boat rigger . . . that I must have done this damage to my leg as I sprinted through the boathouse just moments before.

How long ago was that now? I apparently don't even care enough to bleed. I observe from a great distance, feeling nothing.

This time I'm having an **OUT**-of-boat experience . . .

Eventually a team manager gathers me up and binds my leg. He's horrified, but there's no time to go to the hospital or I'll miss the second shift.

The team comes back. The third varsity stroke, a tall, soft-spoken sophomore named Joe Lehman, never has there been a nicer guy, but whose body was putty to my steel, is sitting in *my* seat, and everybody's excited!

The varsity boat is finally *moving!*

. . . OH, WHERE IS THE JUSTICE? . . .

Fred Leonard directs me to the six seat in the JV.

Never again will I see the inside of *my* first boat.

Me, the varsity stroke since forever, the top weight lifter, no one more hard core, now relegated to the JV. How could this happen?

How could this happen to *me?*

I was even supposed to be co-captain of this crew, for Heaven's sake. My good friend, Captain Larry Walsh, our natural leader, had already served as captain for our junior year when, one fine spring day a year ago, he came up to me out of the blue and said he would decline nomination for our senior year and instead propose that Saul Berman and I serve as his worthy successors.

I can't tell you how touched I was.

But when the time finally came and Larry was nominated, he remained silent, and he was re-elected by acclamation.

Hell, even *I* voted for him.

Days later, when the shock had worn off, I asked Larry what happened. He told me he decided it might look bad on his résumé if he hadn't succeeded himself.

I can't tell you how touched I was.

And now *this!*

After practice, with my leg still bandaged, I go to Fred, in whom I have placed my trust for three years, Fred Leonard, a father figure of sorts to me, and beg him to tell me what I am doing wrong, what Joe is doing better than me, because no matter what it is, I will adapt, I will learn, I will change, I will do whatever it takes, I will earn back my seat.

Fred is terribly embarrassed. He tells me I'm not doing *anything* wrong. I'm just not a boat mover, not like Joe turned out to be. Or maybe it's just some chemistry thing between Joe and the rest of the boat. He can't explain it . . . and he can't help me.

* * * * *

Looking back on that day, I can tell you I was devastated. I felt betrayed by my own sport. I had given it everything, and it had turned on me.

But I didn't feel betrayed by Fred. No, it seems to me that somehow there was genius at work in his looking all the way to the third boat, to Joe Lehman of all people, to replace me. I knew if Fred could have helped me, he would have, and if Fred couldn't, I knew nobody could.

Many times I have retold this story as a coach, each successive team of mine gathered around the campfire, feeling my pain. A host of lessons to be learned here. A morality tale. And every time I have retold it I have called it "The Curse of the JV Scar."

Incidentally, I will carry the mark of this experience till my dying day, not only on my soul but also on my thigh.

The scar. It's still there. Just ask me. I'll be happy to show it to you.

The Wings of Angels

It nearly destroyed me that day to be found wanting by my sport of rowing . . . and with no explanation. My life was spinning. I was delirious. Why, just nine months earlier, I had transcended ordinary experience. I had touched the divine at the Royal Canadian Henley Regatta.

In those days, lightweights in the U.S. had to average 150 pounds during the summer, but in Canada you had your choice: 145 or 155. So in the summer of 1966 Fred splits his squad in two, packing the 155-pound group with all of my Penn varsity teammates, while I and a bunch of younger guys are chosen to lose an additional ten pounds.

I can't quite remember how I pulled off making it all the way to 145, as off-season I am a solid 170 without a lot of body fat.

Or why me?

Enough to say that I dwelled in the Land of Anorexia for several eventful days and weeks . . .

* * * * *

We arrive in St. Catherines, Ontario, and things start well for us from the beginning. First of all, we're actually here! Remember in 1965 we had to skip this most fun regatta in the world because somebody had to work, and that probably cost us the Nationals that year!

Now we find Mack Sennett comedies on the tube at the Hotel Leonard (no relation to Fred, but a good omen nonetheless), and a slot car track just down the street. Plenty to keep our minds off our stomachs, and we all make weight.

> *"Well, Stanley, this is another fine mess*
> *you've gotten me into!"*
>
> - Oliver Hardy

Life is good.

In our very first race I stroke our 145-pound four without cox'n to a surprising and unexpected victory. We can't seem to get off the start line with anybody, but what the Hell, we move from last to first like a knife through butter. During the last 500 meters it's close, but we still have time for an in-boat discussion about our steering.

photo credit: the Mallory Collection

Collecting our Canadian Henley 145-Pound Coxless Four Gold Medals.

Before this summer, I had seen cox fours. Four guys with one oar each, a cox'n along to steer and cheer. But in a coxless four, who steers? Well, turns out one of the rowers, for us this day it's the bow man, one of the rowers has wires from the rudder attached to his foot stretcher. Twist his foot, and the boat responds.
Voila!
Pretty slick.
This athlete is referred to as "the toe," and it takes a lot of skill to row AND look around to see where you're going AND use the rudder.

38

Coxless fours are a common sight in Canada and Europe but rare in America.

And this day I decide I like coxless fours a great deal. Yessirree.

Our second day is to be a much sterner test. The start of our four with cox'n race is scheduled exactly forty minutes after the start of the eight race!

Let's see. I got an 800 in math on my College Boards. It takes more than six minutes just to row the eight race. If we win, and we plan to, after all, we haven't lost yet, if we win we will have to catch our collective breath and then paddle over to the grandstand for the medal presentation. That will take maybe ten minutes. Then we cross the course to the docks, where our other shell will be waiting for us. Climb out of the eight and into the cox four. Tie in. Another ten minutes. What's that leave? Maybe thirteen minutes to row 2,000 meters back to the starting line and maneuver into the stake boats before the official begins to poll the lanes for our next race?

Hell, we'll have to row back up the course at near race pace just to make it!

Our eight is an okay group, but, as I have said, not exactly overflowing with talent, and not that much had been expected from us when we left Philadelphia.

Lot of youth, some experience. Mostly youth.

The stern holds the same four guys who won the day before and who will be racing twice in forty minutes today. Before this weekend, I hardly knew all their names.

After this weekend, I will *still* hardly know all their names.

Immediately behind me is Tom Cassel, a sophomore from the Penn JV and just coming into his own as a rower. He wears glasses and is still a bit shy, but he is a superb athlete, already deceptively strong, and an excellent slot car driver.

Next comes Geoff Holmes, from last spring's Penn Freshman Lightweight Crew, blond hair, not very powerful, don't remember ever having had a conversation with him, before or since.

John Hanson, a high school kid from Haverford School on the Main Line in the Philadelphia, completes the set. He has gotten a lot of teasing for being so young. We have given him a somewhat bawdy version of his last name and used it with such regularity that I have nearly forgotten that he came into the world with a "real" name.

Yesterday he was our toe, and I hadn't completely agreed with the way he steered the straight four race, but he hadn't backed down either, and he got us over the line in first place.

Good for him.

Not even a chance for steering problems today, though, because the now sadder and wiser 1965 buoy-veteran Saul Berman, co-uncaptain of the Penn Lightweight Crew along with me, will be our cox'n.

As usual when he's dieting, Saul shows up crabby. He's almost as tall as the rest of us, and this year he's lost even more weight than we have.

Saul is an odd guy, very serious, curiously distant. We're now roommates back home, but, as you know, I am a history of art major.

Saul's studying accounting.

He's chief justice of the university judiciary. I minor in philosophy and fraternities.

Oil and water.

While the rest of us are having a serious discussion about whether enough time has gone by for a full re-evaluation of the historically underrated contribution of Shemp Howard to the Three Stooges, Saul's probably debating within himself the economic impact of the investment tax credit.

Oil and water, but still fine friends. The first time I ever tasted horseradish was at Seder at Saul's house.

Saul Berman, an Ichabod Crane of a cox'n, gaunt and bony and angular, backs our eight into the start area, and all the best American and Canadian crews line up beside us. Just like yesterday, we come off the line in last place, but Saul deftly moves us through to take the lead in the final 500 meters. Saul wants to cruise it in and conserve energy for the next race, but I insist on a thirty-stroke final burst.

I am in no mood to take chances. After all, we are about to win our second Canadian Henley championship in less than twenty-four hours!

We cross the line open water ahead.

Over to the stands. Collect our medals. Haul ass back to the dock.

Then things start going south on us.

40

I'm antsy to get going again, afraid we won't make it back to the start line in time, and I'm hungry to make it three wins in a row. In fact, I'm just plain hungry.

It's a hot, sunny day, and in this era before Gatorade, our teammates hand us cups of hot bouillon out of a thermos so that we can replace the fluids and minerals we've sweated out during the previous race. Tom is standing next to me, animatedly describing to the 155s, in epic fashion and form, our stirring sprint in the eight, yadda, yadda, yadda . . . when he burns his lip on the bouillon and drops his cup. A dollop of the hot liquid hits the dock and rebounds all the way up into my eye.

Now, I'm not just impatient, I am Polyphemus, and Tom Cassel is Nobody!

On that note we shove off and begin to make our way back to the start line. Our opponents are already there.

Saul and I sit in the stern of the boat facing one another while he orchestrates the bitching. Everybody's got an opinion. We all argue about everything and nothing, we even argue about arguing, the entire way back up the race course.

In spite of ourselves, we barely make it in time to spin the boat and back into the start floats.

The gun goes off, and five of the six boats leap forward. Everybody . . . but us!

Holy cow! We're last. Dead Last. DFLWFB!

(As in "way back." You figure the rest out.)

That's okay. At least the infernal complaining has ended. Even Saul quiets down after our racing start is complete . . .

Wait a minute.

You know, we may be tired as Hell and all alone behind everybody else, but the boat actually feels pretty good. Smooth and swinging and light. Who cares about the other boats? Who cares about the race? Not me. I'm rationalizing: I've already won my fair share today.

But, what the Hell, I suggest to Saul that he tell everyone how good it feels. As usual, he's looking past me and not listening. Probably considering Keynesian economics or something.

Four hundred meters gone. You know, I think I can start to sense a couple of boats coming back to us. And our boat feels *really* good. The stroke is climbing. Effortlessly. I feel like a million bucks.

"Saul! Tell them!"

Five hundred meters, and Saul wakes up. We have moved from sixth to fourth, and all fatigue, all weight, all the cares of the world have fallen far behind us.

At 600 meters we are pressing for second. Saul is in full song. His hoarse, raspy voice sounds farther and farther away as he tries to put into words what we already know:

We are Gods this day!

The four of us manning the oars propel Saul into the lead at 800 meters. By the 1,000, our opponents have disappeared behind us. The race has lost its relevance. We are flying with the wings of angels to the very gates of Heaven.

The sky is an impossible blue. Have trees ever been so green?

"Saul, is that actually a smile on your face?

"Saul, is this great or what?

"Listen. I have time now. Explain this 'debits on the left, credits on the right' stuff to me again.

"And this is supposed to be interesting, right?

"Are there accountants in Heaven, Saul?"

If anyone cared to look, the other boats are now water bugs on the horizon. How they scramble. Why do they hurry so? I observe from a cloud far above. I am a *putto*, a little angel on a painted ceiling in a Baroque church in Rome . . .

The *ultimate* out-of-boat experience!

The noise of the grandstand is growing close. I hardly notice.

I wonder if I will want to stop at the finish . . .

. . . or keep on rowing forever.

We cross the line, and something turns me around to make sure everyone has sensed the same magic I have felt.

Their faces glow.

Eventually the other crews creak and crash over the line, collapse briefly, and then slink away. Waves of indescribable joy wash over our entire boat.

It was the best I ever felt. In my life. Before or since. That memory will stay with me until I die.

photo credit: the St. Catherines Standard

1966 Undine Barge Club Canadian Henley 145-Pound Champions
Top: Coach Fred Leonard, stroke Peter Mallory, Tom Cassel, Geoff Holmes, John Hanson, Manager Joe Burk"e" Bottom: A. Pismo Clam, Henry Ingersoll, cox'n Saul Berman, Mahatma Kane Jeeves, bow Al Casale

Incidentally, thirty-four years later, me, Mr. Art History, Joe Jock, I have become a CPA, just like my good friend Saul Berman.

Serves You Right

The memory of my perfect race in St. Catherines the previous summer continues to haunt me this winter day of the JV Scar in 1967 as I drag my bandaged thigh across the Penn dock to take my seat in the second boat.

> *"Walk this way, stupid!"*
> - old vaudeville gag

How could the Gods have been with me in Canada and then deserted me so today?

But, you know, in some ways it makes sense. None of us knew how we'd done it in St. Catherines, how everything could have come together so perfectly for one magical moment.
And none of us could conjure up the magic again, not even the very next day.

That next morning our four with cox'n goes out again.
Same exact boat. Up a class.

> *"It's showtime!"*
> - Beetlejuice

We row a fine race but lose narrowly to a good crew from Detroit. If we could have rowed a second *perfect* race we would have won by a mile, but our godhead had vanished as mysteriously as it had arrived, and we are merely competent humans again.

We finish the Royal Canadian Henley Regatta with another win and another second that very afternoon. Four championships and two seconds out of six events over three days. Not too shabby.

But just one perfect race . . . and a sense of loss, for now we know what is *possible!*

* * * * *

44

When we return from St. Catherines to our own country, Saul, Tom and I become the heart of Fred's best shot at a 1966 U.S. championship on the Schuylkill two weeks later.

He teams us with Martin Dominguez from the Penn Varsity, whose father teaches architecture at Cornell. Very congenial, the father, very aristocratic fellow. Refugee from Havana. Got out when Castro took over. Met us all that very spring when we raced in Ithaca.

Think of this. If I'd gone to Cornell I might have taken a course from Dr. Dominguez and never met Martin.

I might even be an architect today!

Hmm!

In another life, that might have been okay with me. Never much liked Martin. Nobody else quite understood why I didn't like him. Me neither. Didn't care. Didn't like him.

But he is a fine oarsman, and I am happy to be stroking with Martin behind me in the three seat.

The stern pair of last spring's Penn Lightweight Varsity reunited!

Oh my!

The two man is Al Campbell, another Haverford School kid, but big and strong this time. No John Hanson he. Al towers over me and has trouble making weight.

Tom moves to bow, saying he will beat us all to the finish line.

Line up at the start. Same deal. Last off the line. Row through the field. Tougher field this time.

No magic, either, just a very strong boat.

As mere mortals, but very good ones, we enter the last 500 meters having risen to second and moving like a freight train on the St. Catherines Rowing Club entry in first.

We still have plenty of time as I up the rating and begin our final surge to the lead. Half a length and closing.

Fred is watching us from the other side of the river, following the race in his car. With a quarter mile to go we disappear from his view behind Peter's Island for thirty strokes or so. He says to the others with him, "It will all be decided by the time we see them again."

Thus spake the Oracle at Delphi.

Back in the boat, the margin is down to a deck and closing fast.
Sweet victory . . .

And then it's over. Before we can reach the end of the island, Al catches a crab, and we must scramble to salvage a second.

"Catches a crab." An oar caught under the water at the end of the stroke. As if held by the claws of a giant crab, I suppose that's how the expression got started.
Sounds like a joke, a witticism.
No . . .
More like one of those black-and-white fifties "B" horror movies with enormous spiders and lizards.
"It's no use, General. The giant mutant crab rose from the depths, grabbed that poor man's oar, and then disappeared as quickly as it came. Bullets bounced right off of it."

A silver medal. Again, no photo. Again, two places in the race . . .

Two silvers in two years now at the U.S. Nationals, and we should have won both times. Dammit!

* * * * *

A few years ago I heard that Al Campbell had been killed in a plane crash. I caught myself mouthing, "Serves you right, you son of a . . ." before I caught myself.
Rest in peace, Al. If not for that crab I might never have stuck to my journey, might have abandoned my quest, might never have written this book.

* * * * *

And so I, four-time Canadian Henley champion and double U.S. silver medalist, surrender to the Curse of the JV Scar and finish my collegiate career in the Penn second boat.
No third varsity letter.
No Penn Varsity Blanket.

46

Weak and Weaker

The Curse of the JV Scar touches not just me. My best friend on the crew, Bob Harrison, a legend in his own mind, who, in Napoleonic fashion, that very year has crowned himself "Mr. Bulk-Giant" in honor of his prowess pumping iron, is demoted from first to second boat along with me, he being replaced by a sweet beanpole of a fellow named Henry Ingersoll, part of my 145-Pound eight in Canada, the other half of the former third boat stern pair with Joe Lehman.

photo credit: the Mallory Collection

Bob Harrison (pre-bulk giant), me (pre-scar), Martin Dominguez (prehensile tail).

And so Mallory and Harrison, the two strongest weight lifters on the squad, find themselves replaced by Lehman and Ingersoll, co-stars of the movie *Weak and Weaker*.

47

I wanted an explanation!!!!

But none was forthcoming.

I couldn't accept that. And thus I continued my decades-long quest for an answer, an explanation, for peace, for resolution, for redemption.

And now you know why I am writing this book.

> *"My pathway led by confusion boats*
> *Mutiny from stern to bow.*
> *Ah, but I was so much older then.*
> *I'm younger than that now."*
> — Robert Allen Zimmerman

But I can't leave 1967 without telling you how it all turned out that year. The Lehman/Ingersoll varsity boat was absolutely terrific that first day and only got faster.

* * * * *

At the beginning of the season the Cornell Lightweights come to Philadelphia to race us on the Schuylkill. Their first boat arrives hungry, having lost to Harvard in the previous year's Eastern Sprints. My old prep school friend, Chris Williams, is stroking them. Joe, Henry, Captain Larry and the rest of the crew give them a Hell of a race and lose only narrowly in the last 200 meters.

No question Fred has made the right decision.

Bob Harrison and I had sulked a bit in our new roles in the Greek chorus, exiled to Elba, but by the time the stitches are removed from my thigh, we have both knuckled down to the job at hand.

This day, we row out to our race against the Cornell JV with the words "Lightweight Rowing's Strongest Weight Lifting Pair" written on athletic tape and stuck to the sides of the shell next to our seats.

At least we still have our pride intact . . .

Despite (?) our best efforts in the five and six seats, the JV doesn't swing very well. We haven't been real close to the varsity in practice, and so in our race we are quite pleased when we fall only three of a length behind Cornell after 1,500 meters.

During our entire collegiate careers, none of us had ever been this close to the men from Ithaca this late in a race.

And so with 500 meters to go we are comfortable with losing . . . but excited about finishing respectably.

Our cox'n, Saul Berman (Yes, Saul, too, has made that sentimental journey to the JV. It appears my illness, my condition, is *infectious!)* Saul calls for a perfunctory sprint, and, what the Hell, we give him a perfunctory response.

Well, what do you know?

We come flying up and lose by only a foot at the line. We are absolutely astonished! Too astonished to be disappointed that we have come so very, very close without actually winning.

We come to rely on that sprint. Yessirree. Later in the season we actually catch MIT after falling a full two lengths back.

This day we return to the Penn dock from our race with Cornell to a pretty happy Fred Leonard. Two narrow losses in the varsity and JV, and our freshmen have actually won.

Against *Cornell!*

Good start to the season. No question about *that!*

Now, as I have already mentioned, every collegiate race in our country includes a traditional wager, every member of the winning crew receiving as booty the racing shirt worn by the corresponding member of the losing crew. In a three-boat race the winners receive two shirts. At a championship the winners can go home with a whole caboose-full.

In my life I never won a Cornell shirt. Supplied Penn shirts to a host of Cornellians over the years, starting in 1964 with that fellow I later would run into in Yosemite, and ending, I can report in retrospect, on this particular weekend my senior year.

Chris Williams comes over to me as I am stripping off my racing shirt and handing it to my victorious Cornell JV counterpart, a pleasant fellow named Billy Brown, sounds like Buster Brown's little brother, better yet a kid in the "Little Rascals" comedy shorts, don't you think?

One of Spanky's buddies.

compliments me on our performance but says a
.ty teammates are interested in discussing with Bob and
st Weight Lifting Pair" sign of ours.

.it to call one particular fellow over, when I beg him to
.d me to preserve our fantasy.

aven's sake, it's all we have!

Chris acquiesces, and so I will have to wait twenty-two more years to meet Eric Loberg, a man destined to add spice to my life.

* * * * *

That JV of ours turns out to have a very satisfying season. We don't lose another race after Cornell, and with the benefit of hindsight, I can report to you one special happenstance from our very next race.

That next Saturday it is Yale's and Columbia's turns to fall victims to our new-found withering sprint. And so I win a Yale shirt and a Columbia shirt, but that's not the interesting thing. The interesting thing is the Columbia guy who gives me his shirt is James Simon Kunen, who later will write *The Strawberry Statement, Notes of a College Revolutionary*, a very entertaining book about how he used to sneak out of the university president's office, where he was participating in the Columbia student strike, how he used to sneak out through underground passages to go to crew practice.

They even made a movie out of his book. Kunen went Hollywood.

I won his shirt that day in 1967, but at the time, neither of us realized we would both eventually get around to writing books about rowing.

Too bad. I'm sure we would have had a lot more to say to each other that day, if we had only known.

Is this a small world or what?

By the way, apparently you can still special-order *The Strawberry Statement*.

I recommend it.

Harvard's Secret Weapon

That JV of ours enters the Eastern Sprint Championships seeded third behind still undefeated Cornell . . . and an undefeated Harvard JV.

Before the qualifying heats, as the various JV lightweight boats mill around the starting area, our eyes are searching for Harvard, the only crew we hadn't raced yet. Our friends from Cornell will be with us in Heat Two, and we know we will beat them this day.

But Harvard . . .

Look! There they are, sitting fifty meters away, waiting for their Heat One.

The other half of "Lightweight Rowing's Strongest, etc., etc." is right behind me, and Bob Harrison is enthralled, even obsessed with all things Harvard.

In 1967 Harvard is the fashion capital of American rowing. By all accounts their shirts should be "Harvard Crimson," you know, a real red like Cornell's. Isn't that what "crimson" means to you?

But their traditional color is actually an indescribable, dark, maroon . . . something.

And if you give them a chance, Harvard shirts run. They fade. That is, if you can hold on to them long enough.

And that's the point! At Penn, most Saturdays we sport brand-spanking-new shirts, the creases still in the sleeves, issued to us in plastic that very day . . . because we've *lost* our last shirts just the Saturday before.

Old shirts mean you haven't lost in a while.

And these Harvard guys across the lake have faded shirts. *Ergo:* undefeated. Do you think a couple of guys might even have helped the effect along with just a drop or two of bleach along the way?

Perhaps.

And the pants. They start out a creamy off-white, but with the shirts running and rigger grease ever present . . .

Well you can just imagine.

Harvard has already made faded and grubby a fashion statement in rowing. Our preppy sport has anticipated "grunge" by thirty years!

Meanwhile, the outside world is also beginning to impinge upon the insular world of rowing. By 1968, the year of Medgar Evers and Martin King and Bobby Kennedy, Harvard oarsmen will begin to sport beards and protest the Vietnam War.

Even now, a year earlier, hair is getting longer on the Charles River, well before the phenomenon will spread to Boathouse Row.

Now long hair can be a hassle in rowing. Flops down over the eyes. Drips with sweat. Harvard guys have a solution: bandannas. Often dirty ones. Goes with the faded shirts.

And so the fashion statement is complete!

As we await the Eastern Sprints qualifying heats, Bob Harrison, undefeated for four consecutive weeks now and smelling the part, in conscious or unconscious *homage* to the Harvard culture, has wrapped a Harvard-style bandanna around his head to compliment the oldest, the dirtiest shirt he has ever worn in his collegiate career . . . and he is squinting toward the Crimson boat.

"How can they be so good?" he asks.

Across the board, they have beaten our mutual opponents by about a length more than we have. They must have a secret weapon, an unfair advantage. After all, no one could have trained any harder than we have.

(And I'm sure he is thinking that no JV could be as good as *us!* What with all the "varsity caliber" oarsmen in our boat . . . you know . . . Right?)

"What the heck are they doing? Hey, it looks like they are passing something up and down the boat . . . Are they eating it? Something hidden in a napkin? Maybe it's *drugs!*"

Bob is incensed. The unfairness of it all! We all strain our eyes to identify this "substance" that must be the nefarious secret of Harvard's invincibility.

The first heat is called to the line. Harvard moves off. "Look!" says Bob, "There's something floating in the water."

"LET'S GO GET THE EVIDENCE!"

We paddle over. Bob fishes a paper napkin from the lake. He opens it. We all hold our breath . . .

"It's a lemon peel," says Paul Garnerberg derisively, looking over Bob's shoulder from the four seat. "It's just a lemon peel, for Heaven's sake. Harvard's unfair advantage is *lemons!*"

Bob Harrison says no more that morning.

Harvard wins their heat. We win ours.

That afternoon, we return to the starting area for the final. As we sit and wait, Bob has something in his hand. He is hiding it. "What's going on, Bob?"

Silence.

I can't resist. I grab for it. It's a lemon. My best friend, in his Harvard bandanna, is sucking a lemon.

Perhaps thanks to that lemon, we row a magnificent race, pass three boats in the last ten strokes, a final sprint for the ages. We beat everybody . . . that is, everybody but Harvard.

Perhaps they have better lemons.

And our varsity? Second to Cornell. How 'bout that?

Bravo, Joe Lehman and Henry Ingersoll!

Chris Williams and his Cornell teammates are headed for the Thames Cup at the Royal Henley Regatta in England as U.S. Eastern Lightweight Varsity Champions. I am *green* with envy!

Bravo Cornell!

Meanwhile, our freshman lightweights have beaten everybody, and with that, Penn wins the E.A.R.C. lightweight team trophy!

The Jope Cup!

Bravo Fred Leonard!

Years later, Bob Harrison finally makes it to graduate school at his beloved Harvard.

Bravo Bob!

And Henry Ingersoll, who used to be neighbors with Ethel Kennedy in McLean, Virginia, now, decades later, he's neighbors with *me* in Del Mar, California. Is this a small world or what?

He never calls.

"We're family, Henry!"

"I'm in the phone book!"

Some Little Kid

I graduate in May of 1967, and my life takes me around the world and back, but I return to Philadelphia and Undine for the summer of 1968. It was a lightweight eight for me in 1965, a lightweight cox four in 1966. This year it will be a lightweight quad, four guys with two oars each and no cox'n, and we're returning to Orchard Beach, but sadly without Fred Leonard. No more summer coaching for him.

Our loss.

Simple story here. Again we never took a picture. To write this book I even had to ask Tom Cassel if he had been in the boat.

Turns out he was, and he even had an old, faded newspaper clipping from the *New York Times!*

(That's what we all are now, incidentally. Old, faded newspaper clippings.)

Me in bow, John Cantrill in two, Cassel in three, my old 1965 Nationals Eight teammate Don Callahan in stroke.

I wonder if he remembers.

"We're family, Don!

"I'm in the phone book! Del Mar, California."

That year without Fred was to be our last hurrah. The end of an era for Penn Lightweights at Undine.

What happened in our swansong? We four men, a good boat, the favorites according to the *New York Times*, we got beat, fair and square.

No buoys. They were gone by then, thank Heavens, and no crabs, either. Just a better boat from Detroit Boat Club, a bunch of guys from the 1965 eight that had beaten our buoy-challenged boat. Beat us this time by eleven seconds. Not much of a race for them.

I wonder if they even remember.

Hell of a race for us.

* * * * *

With about 600 meters to go and us resigned to second, I suddenly realize we have wandered a bit off course, thanks to me, me being the "toe," it being my responsibility to row, steer and feel sorry for myself simultaneously . . . and we're headed straight for a dock.

Crank in a big course change!

When I straighten us back out, we find a boat from Upper Merion Boat Club, five miles up the Schuylkill River from the rest of Boathouse Row, a boat from Upper Merion is suddenly nipping at our heels.

Upper Merion?

Impossible!

These guys are jokes!

The bow man is a guy named Vince Bindo. He has rowed in Philadelphia forever and never won anything. He's ancient! A joke! Over thirty, for Heaven's sake!

(An uncomfortable memory for me today, now that I am nearly a quarter century older than Vince was then!)

And the boat is stroked by some little kid.

A little kid, for Heaven's sake!

What's his name? Billy Belden? He must be a future world champion if he can carry a derelict like Vince Bindo down the course and challenge us in the National Championships.

"Don't you know we are the favorites, Billy Belden?"

U.S. silver medal number three.

Oh my!

Musical Interlude

In the fall of 1970, three years after graduation, I rejoin Fred Leonard at Penn, my *alma mater*, as his Freshman Lightweight Coach . . . and renew in earnest my journey toward redemption from the JV Scar.

That year I share coaching duties with my good friend and 1968 quad teammate, John Cantrill. In 1966 he went 155 in Canada while I had gone 145, and so he missed our perfect race, but he kept his seat in the Penn Varsity the year Bob and Saul and I were overthrown, so he earned the Penn Varsity Blanket I never did. He makes sure it's on my bed every time I visit him.

How considerate!

John Cantrill is a man of rare wit, a talented mimic, and a forever friend and fellow aficionado of one particular 1960s television show. He has only one problem. It's his wife. She thinks she's a refrigerator.

So why doesn't he take her to a psychiatrist?

He would . . . but he doesn't want to let the food spoil.

> *"Show me Lassie's puppy eating cantaloupe . . .*
> *. . . and I'll show you a melon collie baby."*
> - Words of Wisdom

One of my most vivid memories of John Cantrill occurs while we were still undergraduates.

Ever seen rowing tanks? The idea is to provide water for rowers to train in during the winter months when rivers and lakes are icebound. Yale's tanks are in a monumental space in a cathedral of a gymnasium. Harvard's are right in the boathouse. MIT's are state of the art.

(And what would you expect from Massachusetts Institute of TECHNOLOGY?)

In all of them, the water actually moves by you, recirculates as you sit and row. Very sophisticated, with turbines and venturis and . . .

You know, I have no idea how they work. Somebody turns them on, and off you go. They're awesome.

Not at Penn. Philadelphia doesn't get enough ice to justify that much expense, so no moving-water tanks for us. Instead, still-water tanks.

Those three words cannot begin to describe the horror of still-water tanks. Like rowing with your boat still tied to the dock. No. Like rowing in concrete, arms aching with effort. Add the ambiance of a gymnasium basement, no, a sub-basement, low ceilings, rough concrete, dirt floors, actually *behind* the ROTC rifle range . . . and then you enter the chamber itself, essence de mold and mildew . . .

A Proustian memory washes over me . . . and my crotch is starting to itch.

* * * * *

When Olympic champion Ted Allison Nash arrives at Penn to coach the freshmen heavyweights (Remember Dexter Bell?), he spruces up the tanks with paint and polish, with flags and inspirational signs. It all seems a bit silly to us lightweights, as we play our roles as boathouse court jesters. Ted takes everything so seriously, even the tanks.

But, thanks to Ted Nash, great crews emerge from these tanks every spring. No arguing with success. But his signs . . .

One day Ted leaves on the blackboard the following inspirational saying:

> *"Pain makes cowards of us all.*
> *Take 10 hard ones and beat it!"*
>   - Ted A. Nash

I turn my back for a second, and it reads,

> *"Pain makes cowards of us all.*
> *Take a hard one and beat it 10 times!"*
>   - A.N. Onymous

John has chalk dust on his fingers. We get the Hell out of there.

* * * * *

John and I learn a lot by coaching together. I saw him single-handedly save the lives of nine people on the very brink of being swept over the dam in an eight one night after dark.

I'm *not* exaggerating!

John Cantrill's a real-life hero.

And John and I turn out a pretty good crew that year. Yessirree. With names like Magic Man and Saltman and Boltman and Alt Man and Space Man. Terrific year, and with no loss of life, thank Heavens, and only a single *Twilight Zone* episode at Columbia.

Norman Hildesheim, named after a beautiful village in Germany with a beautiful cathedral, in 1971 Norman Hildesheim is the Freshman Lightweight Crew Coach for Columbia University. That year it is our turn to travel to the august Columbia Boathouse on the Harlem River at the top of Manhattan to race Norman's crew.

That year they beat us. Cross the finish line first. Parade around their campus the next week with *our* shirts on. Two horizontal red stripes across the chest, a blue "P" with an oar through it over each of their hearts, hearts bursting with *perfidy*, I can assure you.

* * * * *

Columbia.

Turns out that when the tide's running just so, as it is on this particular morning, the current against the crews in the lanes of the racecourse is absolutely brutal.

The official course runs along the left-hand bank, on the Manhattan side of the river, but there are only a few buoys to mark it.

Anyway, right at the start, Norman's crew takes a detour off the race course and over to the right-hand bank, and rows the entire race in still water along the Bronx shore.

Now I'll have you know, at this point the Harlem River is *not* that narrow. So could their course be a mistake? A novice cox'n having trouble steering, for instance?

Get this.

At the 1,000-meter mark Norman's crew encounters the Penn and Columbia JV boats innocently making their way from the boathouse to the start line for their own upcoming race. Norman's crew momentarily detours back onto the race course to avoid certain collision . . . and then returns to the right-hand shore for the balance of our race.

Game. Set. Match.

* * * * *

The next month at the Eastern Sprints? We were thirty-three seconds
faster than they were.
One, one thousand, two, one thousand, three, one thousand . . . .
. . . . (musical interlude) . . . .
. . . . thirty-two, one thousand,
thirty-three, one thousand.

And that just about sums up my opinion of the Columbia University
Crew.

Incidentally, Norman Hildesheim is now the esteemed rowing
correspondent for the *New York Times*. I see him once a year at the San
Diego Crew Classic. Old Home Week.
These days he, too, is an old, faded newspaper clipping.

* * * * *

Was "t-h-i-r-t-y t-h-r-e-e s-e-c-o-n-d-s f-a-s-t-e-r t-h-a-n C-o-l-u-m-
b-i-a" fast enough for us at the Sprints?
Should have been.
In our morning heat, our guys enter the last 500 only half a length
down on Harvard and stroke it in easy, full of confidence.
But in the afternoon, they break a centerbolt as the crews approach
the start. Fearing they'd break the entire foot stretcher during the race
without that bolt, the 1971 Penn Freshman Lightweight Crew dares not
even continue their warm-up while the officials send back to finish area
for a replacement. When it finally arrives, they start the race
immediately. Our guys are freezing.
Did I mention it is pouring rain and forty degrees?
We crab, get off the line in last. In our absence Harvard assumes a
commanding lead.
We pass everybody else, climb back to second by the 1,000, and
move on Harvard the whole way, but it is too late to catch them before
the end. We lose by three-quarters of a length.

photo credit: John Basinski

1971 Penn Freshman Lightweight Crew
Bow Magicman, Space Man, Basher Brown, Rex
Kampefner, Eugene Willia, Mitch Field, Danny Alt Man, stroke Rob Dent Man,
cox'n Bill Clarke.

Today that crew of ours is best remembered for containing Mick Feld, who will earn a seat in the undefeated U.S. Lightweight Eight just one year later as a college sophomore and then go on to be a member of the 1974 World Champion U.S. Lightweight Eight as a college senior.

World champion!

How many of those do you meet in one lifetime?

Periodically John Cantrill and I mention his name to bask in his reflected glory.

Up your Body, Peter!

Throughout my first year of coaching I had been training in a single every morning before graduate school.

Fred wasn't coaching at Undine during the summers any more, so held my nose and moved to Vesper because they had a beautiful lightweight Swiss *Stämpfli* single, the *Ferrari* of racing singles, etc., etc. and a pair of *Stämpfli* sculls for me to use.

(I was still a year away from buying my own beautiful lightweight Swiss *Stämpfli* single.)

Actually, Fred's replacement at Undine, Jim Barker, hated me and all Penn lightweights, knew we preferred Fred, but he seemed to hate me most of all (a man of rare good judgment, you might conclude), and so that beautiful lightweight Swiss *Stämpfli* single at Vesper was just an excuse.

Frankly, the dust of the Undine boathouse hung heavily upon me and I was happy to shake it from my shoes.

The Vesper Sculling Coach that year was a remarkable woman named Anna Tamas (shortened from Tama-Reika) who had won the European singles championship something like ten times in a row for Romania. God, she was impressive!

She is in Heaven now, and so is the man who gave her the coaching job. Suffice it to say she had a smile a mile wide, an accent an inch thick and when she walked into a room the walls shook, and *all* eyes were upon her.

I still wake up in the middle of the night hearing her shout over and over, "Up your body, Peter!"

She would have all her scullers row for miles, literally, miles side-by-side, racing no legs, arms and back only.

"Up your body, Ricky! Up your body, Peter!"

I figured she was yelling at us what her own coach back in Romania must have yelled at her year after year.

Isn't that what all coaches do?

It's certainly the way I started!

But while I was upping my body I never did figure out what she was trying to accomplish, and I got the impression she didn't know either. Generation after generation, we rowers are supposed to do what we're told and not question.

"Their's not to make reply,
Their's not to reason why,
Their's but to do and die:
Into the valley of Death
Rode the six hundred."
- Alfred, Lord Tennyson

Anyway, I win a wristwatch, a big deal in those days, in the intermediate lightweight single at the Independence Day Regatta, still have it as a *souvenir* in a drawer somewhere, though it only actually ran for a year.

(In 1876, Indians took as *souvenirs* pocket watches from the bodies of dead soldiers in the aftermath of the Battle of the Little Big Horn. Thought the ticking they heard was the beating of a hero's heart. Not knowing how to wind a watch, they, too, tired of their *souvenirs* a day later, after the watches ran down.)

But my real goal this year is the lightweight quarter-mile dash at the Nationals, to be held again at Orchard Beach in 1971.

What better place to exorcise my silver medal demons.

The man to beat is Bill Belden.

Where have you heard that name before? Yeah, the little kid in the Upper Merion quad with Vince Bindo. Little kid now become a young man, now rowing for Undine.

Is this a small world or what?

Now Bill ran a 4:10 mile while he was still in high school. In 1970, just for fun, I trained all summer on the track . . . and I ran a 5:02 mile. Kind of puts things in perspective, don't you think?

Surprise, surprise! In a lightweight single Bill Belden can destroy me over 2,000 meters. Hell, he is destined to win the lightweight single world championship in just three more years.

Just like I sort of predicted.

(World champion. How many of those do you meet in one lifetime?)

But believe you me, I am genuinely fast in the dash! I can compete with Bill Belden over a quarter mile!

Bill Belden and I first meet at the Schuylkill Navy Championships in June.

A quarter mile takes fifty-seven strokes. I make it through twenty-five, and then my legs turn to jelly. I am leading, and then Bill is gone.

Just like that.

The cornerstone of my training this summer is stadium stairs, brutal repeat sprints up Franklin Field, one of the many innovations Ted Nash brought to Penn rowing.

I redouble my efforts.

We meet again, Bill and I, on the 4th of July. This time I put three-quarters of a length, a *huge* margin, on him at the start and hold it easily for forty strokes before the wheels again fall off the cart.

It astonishes me how my strength can evaporate in a single instant, but I still have six weeks to go before the Nationals, and now I am sure I have the measure of Bill Belden.

Bill Belden.

And everybody else.

Personal Gold

I train and train and train again. Before or since, I never met a man who could run stadium stairs like I did in 1971, and most of the time in a blue rubber suit with elastic at the neck, wrists and ankles just to help me make weight.

I can still smell that death suit.

I have to weigh in for lightweight races at 150 pounds. I can rather easily reach below 160 by dieting, but the rest has to come off in sweat.

In the summer of 1970 I sometimes wear that rubber suit night and day!

* * * * *

I'm at the Nationals regatta site by Friday morning. I rig my boat, my beautiful Vesper *Stämpfli* single, check out the course in my rubber suit, and check out the scale in my birthday suit. I am 151 ¾ on the official scale by 4:30 that afternoon.

That's close enough. Just exhaling for the next fourteen hours will lose me more than two pounds of water vapor, even if I don't tinkle a single drop in the meantime. I have at least a quarter pound in hand.

I have a Popsicle for dinner, just to wet my whistle. I go to bed at my brother George's apartment in the Bronx. In his refrigerator I place the full bottle of Gatorade, a marvelous new product I will drink as soon as I officially weigh in the next morning.

Middle of the night I am thinking of the heats the next day. Both the lightweight and heavyweight dashes. Lightweight dash first. Should be no problem. Bill Belden is undefeated this summer, and I know I have his number in my stadium-tuned quadriceps muscles. My starts are now at close to 50 strokes per minute. I *settle* to a 44 and take it up at the end. I'm ready . . . if I can just make weight.

I'm mighty thirsty.

I start thinking I'd get back to sleep more easily if I suck on a piece of ice from the refrigerator.

Good idea! I get up and head for the kitchen.

I open the refrigerator door. There's the Gatorade. You know, a sip of Gatorade would be even more effective than a sliver of ice. I open the bottle, take a tiny sip, put the empty bottle back in the refrigerator and close the door. I settle back into bed.

Life is good . . .

. . . empty bottle?

I get back up and look again.

Thirty seconds ago that bottle was full. Uh oh . . .

Not much to be done now. Three hours until my showdown with the scale. I squeeze back into my rubber suit and pray in vain for pee pee.

At dawn I run a bit before hitting the scale. 150 ¾. The guy gives me a break, but we both know there will be no slack allowed tomorrow before the finals. I breathe a sigh of relief, have some toast and honey and head for my boat.

On the water I'm nervous as Hell . . . and GUILTY! I line up for the first heat. No Belden, but two, count them, *two,* former U.S. dash champions among my opponents.

In ten strokes I am open water ahead and easing off. I spend the rest of the race a casual observer, utterly relaxed. I even stop a stroke early by mistake and nearly get nipped as I coast over the line, but no problem. I paddle back for the start of my heavyweight heat.

At most of the summer regattas I have been rowing heavyweight to avoid the dreaded scale, and I've been right in there! Yessirree.

In fact, my ever-improving times should give me a shot at the silver or bronze at the nationals AS A HEAVYWEIGHT!

Are you ready? *Row!*

Back to reality. I look around after ten strokes and I am only a foot or two out of the lead, but I am already gassed from the lightweight race.

And mind fugged.

It wasn't supposed to be this hard. I am not confident. I am rationalizing. The weight loss has obviously sapped my strength, I say. I should be saving it for the lightweight final tomorrow.

I shut down and paddle it in.

I spend the afternoon in my rubber suit in my car on a hot summer day with the radio tuned to WABC and the heater on full blast, chewing gum and spitting.

No more mistakes.

The following morning I hit the scale at 149 ½, focused and fearless.

As I approach the starting line the skies are overcast and the wind is dead calm.

The enormity of the moment presses around me. My silver medal in the eight in 1965 on this very course, my silver medal in the four in 1966, then my silver medal in the quad, again on this very course, in 1968, these boats surround me as adrenaline fuels my heart.

My warm-up racing starts have felt fabulous. Bill Belden is two lanes over. None of us are looking at each other. None of the banter that precedes other races. This is the national finals!

We are aligned.

"Are you ready? *Row!*"

This *can't* be happening!

My port blade is heading straight for the bottom of the lagoon on the very first stroke. My rigger is dragging in the water.

When is the last time I've caught a crab? Why, I have more finesse at the tips of my blades than a surgeon has in the tips of his fingers!

I gather my wits about me and finally get pointed and up to speed, even more adrenaline coursing through my body.

At fifteen strokes I look around. I am dead last, about a length into last, and even *half* a length might as well be a mile when you're a quarter of the way through a dash.

But luckily in a dash there isn't time to think, only to act. I settle into the body of my race, feeling strangely calm. The pressure is off me. No more expectations. Just row my race, like I've done over and over all summer. I think of all the stadium stairs I've run.

I think, "What the Hell?"

Twenty to go now. I look around one more time . . .

I'm in the thick of it. Believe it or not, I have caught almost everybody. No time to ponder the significance of my comeback, no time to ask who is in the lead. I say to myself, "Think of all the work we have done this summer, all the hours in that rubber death suit. In twenty strokes our journey will be complete. What have we got to lose?

"Let's see what we've got for twenty more strokes."

I begin my sprint, and the stroke climbs. No hesitation from my body. I build and build to the line. No more looking. Is this the first time in my life I have had the discipline not to look?

It's over. I've gone fifty-eight strokes instead of the usual fifty-seven to be sure I don't stop early. I drop my blades to the water as the boat keeps gliding. I look around.

There are only two of us left out ahead of the rest, Bill Belden and myself, both coasting side by side, the sound of our oars sliding over the surface of the lagoon the only sound reaching my ears, both of us looking at each other for the first time today. He asks me, "Do you know who won?"

photo credit: G. Barron Mallory

I cannot comprehend the words.

We paddle over to the stands. My Dad. He's actually come to one of my races. He takes a picture, the first photo in four trips to the national finals. Imagine that!

Jim Barker leans down. For years he had been Bill's coach, and in 1968 my coach, too. Now, with me gone to Vesper, he is just Bill's coach.

Jim never thought too much of me as a person, even less of me as a single sculler, and there wasn't much to think about, compared to Bill.

Thought he had seen my best in the dash back on Independence Day. "Incredible race, Pete. I've got to hand it to you. Incredible race."

I don't know what to say . . .

Bill and I wait for the results.

They come. Bill first, me second . . . by two feet. Another silver. That makes four. If they were rings instead of medals, then I've run out of fingers, and I'll have to wear the next one on my thumb!

Oh my!

But, you know, I quickly realize I have proved to myself this day that I am the fastest, the fastest in the country, maybe the fastest ever. Trouble is the gold medal goes, not to the fastest on any given day, but to the boat that crosses the line first.

So often the best don't cross the finish line first!

Bravo Bill Belden! I rowed the last fifty-six strokes at least a length faster than he, but Bill rowed the *first* stroke more than a length faster than me.

Imagine that!

And with all of us so focused on our own boats, I may have been the only guy who even noticed that I crabbed back at the starting line.

But, in the end, who else needed to know? It's the best I've ever rowed. A national silver. A personal gold. Perfect irony.

Too bad it isn't enough to end my personal quest.

Too bad nobody noticed.

* * * * *

The following year I will buy my own brand new *Stämpfli* single from the factory in Zurich. I keep thinking two feet! And with an old boat. Maybe with a new one I can crab and still win! I will name it *"Argent,"* French for the money I'll spent to buy it, Latin for silver, in honor of all the silver medals I have earned . . .

. . . and that is how my brother plays a role in my rowing career.

Argent

My brother George was living in the Bronx that year because he was going to medical school, and that year he took a course in psychology.

One of his assignments was to choose someone interesting and analyze him or her in front of the class as a case-in-point.

You know what's coming. It was me he chose. I became his case study: obsessed with winning, haunted by my destiny to forever finish second:

. . . as an **athlete**, rowing in the second boat my senior year in college, and now wearing my JV letter sweater more than my varsity sweater, second in the nationals in four different years now, and in four different events,

. . . as a **coach**, second in the Eastern Sprints (the first of three straight consecutive redundant second place finishes in a row, I can now report with the benefit of hindsight),

. . . as a **son**, second to my brother in competition for the respect of our father. Oh yes: George the obedient child, me the rebel, he the graduate of Dad's beloved Kent School, me the kid who ran away from Kent in the middle of the night (Didn't I mention that? I'll save that story for another book!), George admitted to Yale, Dad's alma mater (even though he chose Harvard), me wait-listed at Yale (but thrilled to go to Penn), George the doctor-to-be, me only a coach, and on and on.

. . . Now I was even rowing a boat named *Argent!*

When George told me about what he had done, I felt for a moment like my privacy had been violated, my brother discussing my life in class as if I were crazy or something, sort of like I was a bug on a slide under a microscope.

And I think he got some of it wrong, too.

I love competition, but I never resented losing. The essence of competition, the essence of life, is the risk, even the inevitability of losing. Winning has never been my goal. It is the *quest* that gives meaning to life!

An existential man, that's me.

"Il faut imaginer Sisyphe heureux."
                                    - Albert Camus

And while I was often disappointed that my father didn't appreciate me for whom I was, I think that was his loss more than mine.

And I wasn't bitter, oh no, not me . . .

And I always respected my brother, his temperament and accomplishments, but I never wanted to be like him either.

But you know, I always presumed I would have retired from competition after college if only I had kept my seat in the varsity my senior year, I would have retired from competition on the spot if only I had won just one, measly national gold.

As I look back I'm glad I didn't retire, so I have to be glad I was indeed "crazy" enough to catch my brother's eye.

So, bravo George!

And bravo me! Obsession or no, I continued my journey, continued to compete through 1972 and beyond.

Tip the Scales

I learn a great deal more about rowing during my second year of coaching. In my launch I share the Schuylkill with Undine teammate Larry Wittig, who is coaching the freshman crew at his own *alma mater*, Drexel University.

And the new Villanova Freshman Coach is a guy named Mike Vespoli.

The three of us train our crews quite a lot together in this year leading up to the spring of 1972. Larry will reappear in this book. As for Mike, he has done rather well for himself. He rowed in the world champion U.S. eight two years later, and now he makes boats.

Tell him you read about him in this book, and perhaps he'll autograph your next *Millennium* shell for you.

Harvard beat my freshman lightweight crew at the "broken centerbolt" Sprints in 1971. This year it will be Princeton's turn to best us.

* * * * *

This year the Princeton Lightweights are being coached by F. Fairthington Farthington, University of Pennsylvania Class of 1963, a fellow Quaker, thick tortoise-shell glasses, weak jaw-line, shock of hair across his forehead that he regularly brushes aside like Bobby Kennedy used to.

He's seems such a distant fellow, formal, intellectual, intense . . . and intensely preppy.

And having read *Road & Track Magazine* since I was old enough to drive, I can't get over how much Fairthy looks like Masten Gregory, an American who drove grand prix cars in Europe during the 50s, when race car drivers were real men and died with regularity.

Masten Gregory died with regularity and is remembered fondly, even today.

I have actually known who Fairthy Farthington is for quite a long time. When I was a Penn freshmen and had yet to grow tall and robust enough to row, I had actually coxed for him one winter morning in 1964.

Is this a small world or what?

Fairthy was training for the Tokyo Olympics with a bunch of other recent Penn grads. Among them was Frank Shields, who later impregnated his future ex-wife, and out popped Brooke Shields, of all people.

Brooke grew up tall and robust enough to follow in her father's footsteps and row at Penn, but, wouldn't you know it, instead she went to Princeton and pursued other options.

Even if Frank Shields didn't, the famed ventriloquist Edgar Bergen, a regular on the Ed Sullivan Show on Sunday nights on CBS at eight o'clock, the aforementioned Edgar Bergen may not have sent his wooden dummy Charlie McCarthy to college, but he *did* send his real-life daughter Candace to college, and the college they picked was none other than the University of Pennsylvania.

People called her "Cappy" back then, and she was already a famous model who appeared regularly on the covers of *Vogue* and *Mademoiselle* magazines. She became a classmate of mine.

We are fellow Quakers.

I even asked her out once as one of my fraternity pledge tasks. She turned me down, much to my relief, but we had a nice conversation over the phone.

Us being fellow Quakers and all.

Nice person.

Candace Bergen was quite tall, you know, tall and robust enough to row. Just the way Brooke would turn out years later.

But Candace Bergen didn't row either.

Pursued other options, thank you.

But we rowers have persevered without Brooke Shields and Candace Bergen, haven't we?

Without Jennifer Lopez and Tyra Banks either, come to think of it.

My fellow coach Mike Vespoli married the most drop-dead fabulous babe you ever will see, in or out of show business, and she was a *rower*, national class, too. Who needs Brooke Shields? Who needs Cappy Bergen?

Right, Mike?

And I've married a woman, not a rower though, but a woman who looks just like Marilyn Monroe and makes me feel like Joe DiMaggio *should* have felt.

Apparently, there's hope for us all.

"Schwing!"
- Garth Algar

Andrea Mitchell, the network television correspondent, she was also a classmate of Cappy's and mine at Penn. She was another fellow Quaker, though to my knowledge neither Cappy nor I ever ran into her.

Andrea was neither tall nor robust enough to row, but she got over it.

Today she's married to Alan Greenspan, Chairman of the Federal Reserve. Hopefully, now Alan Greenspan also feels like Joe DiMaggio should have felt.

"Andrea Mitchell, NBC News, Washington."
- Andrea Mitchell, NBC News, Washington

* * * * *

Anyway, the Princeton Lightweight Freshmen absolutely crush everyone this spring of 1972. After relegating my fine crew to second place at the Eastern Sprints, they go on to the Intercollegiate Rowing Association Championships and win the freshman *heavyweight* cox four.

To my knowledge a feat unequaled before or since.

They are *that* good. No shame in finishing second to them!

Now Princeton Coach Fairthy Farthington is a singular fellow. He is so shy. He never looks anyone straight in the eye through those glasses of his, but during the course of the year, we become rather good friends, us being fellow Quakers and all.

Fairthy is the first person to get me to really think about coaching as a professional avocation. He introduces me to the writings of Doc Counselman, Indiana University Swim Coach, proponent of applying the tools of science to athletic training, and to Arthur Lydiard, a running coach from New Zealand who stresses long-distance training at sub-maximal levels.

Fascinating!

Every other rowing coach in America is in love with 500-meter interval bursts at higher-than-race pace. Just like the Undine light-weights and Vesper heavyweights in 1965.

Fairthy opens the door to new ideas in my understanding of the sport.

He becomes a father figure of sorts to me.

During this year Fairthy also shares with me his plans to organize a 1972 summer European tour for a U.S. composite lightweight squad: an eight, a coxless four and a single sculler. FISA, the international rowing federation, was on the brink of officially adding these lightweight events to the world championship schedule, and our initiative might just tip the scales for 1973.

Am I interested?

You *bet* I am!

After my performance in the dash the previous summer I have forgotten all about the JV Scar, about boat movers and boat stoppers. I am 27, running and lifting like never before, and even spinning that new fangled invention from Australia, the ergometer, as well as any lightweight around, anyone except my former freshman phenomenon Mick Feld.

Mick is in a class by himself in America.

Nevertheless, I am anxious to take on the world, and with Mick in my boat.

Fairthy arranges everything: the schedule of regattas in Germany, Austria and Denmark, the selection camp at Harvard, European transportation, lodging, everything, but he can't actually participate himself. Some personal or family conflict.

Fairthy even gets Steve Gladstone, the Harvard Lightweight Coach, undefeated for many years by now (Harvard having now long supplanted Cornell as the premier lightweight program in America) he gets Steve Gladstone to be in charge of selection before we leave the States.

Even gets me to agree to be rower/rigger/manager/*VW combi* driver in Europe.

Concierge, if you will.

"À votre service, monsieur."

76

Died With His Boot Stretchers On

When the camp convenes in Cambridge, I am the oldest, most experienced, most versatile man present. My ergo scores are more than competitive. And after 1971, I'm in a class by myself on stadium stairs. I'm comfortable on port and starboard, experienced from bow to stroke, from pairs to eights, I'm even one of the country's better single scullers.

By the time I get there, the early arrivals have done a head count and suggest I shoot for the starboard side. There seems to be an overabundance of superstars who have stroked their college varsities on port.

Fine with me.

Every morning I row starboard in team practice under an interim coach while we all await Gladstone's arrival.

Every afternoon I practice my single with a group of local Charles River scullers led by former world doubles silver medalist Sy Cromwell, a man who is up in Heaven now.

* * * * *

Ever meet Seymour Cromwell? A gentle man. He died of cancer just a few years after we rowed together.

Our loss. I hardly knew him, and I miss him terribly.

Last saw him in the stands at the Montreal Olympics.

The great love in Sy's life was Gail Pierson, but she wasn't yet his wife when Sy and I were sculling on the Charles.

Coincidentally, Gail and her mother would be counted among my absolute best friends in Europe in the weeks just after I left Cambridge that very same summer of '72, Gail and I the two American single scullers at all these regattas so far from home.

Well, four years later in the stands in Montreal, Gail was leaping all over my case because I hadn't been more grateful to have assigned to my team in San Diego some fifty-plus-pound Olympic Development Committee training pig of a single that nobody else wanted and I didn't need, and because I hadn't dropped everything and driven 1,000 miles to pick the darn thing up, blah, blah, blah.

Sy suggested to his dear wife that life was too short to waste any of it being angry.

"Way too short, dear."

Words to live by.

As I said, a gentle man. Rest in peace, Seymour Cromwell.

You know how Sy figured out he was sick? That summer he rowed with me his 500-meter times weren't coming down the way they should have.

Now there's a man who died with his boot stretchers on!

The Ides of March

Steve Gladstone's 1971 Harvard Lightweight Varsity was generally acknowledged to have been the fastest lightweight crew in the history of mankind, winners at Henley, broke six minutes flat over 2,000 meters in Lucerne, Switzerland, with the equipment of that era, boats and oars fifty percent heavier than those of today.

"The Super Boat," that's what we called them. Everyone idolized these guys. I even did a silk-screen rendering of them thundering off the line at Henley.

When I went to JKF airport to pick up my beautiful new *Stämpfli* single, just arrived from Europe, there was another *Stämpfli* single right next to mine with Super Boat bow man Phin Sprague's name on it.

I hung around for a while, hoping he might show up just so I could meet him.

I gave up after an hour. Never did meet Phin Sprague.

art credit: Peter Mallory

The Harvard Super Boat
Phin Sprague, Andy Narva, Eph King, Tony Brooks, Jim Richardson, Chuck Hewitt, Dickie Moore, Dave Harmon, cox'n Fred Yalaurius.

I was destined to meet Tony Brooks in Europe that very summer of 1972. Get this! He made the Olympic team as a heavyweight!

I was destined also to meet Moore and Richardson. Good men. Chuck Hewitt and I would become fine friends. He also made the 1972 Olympic team as a heavyweight, and the straight four he rowed in Munich would eventually provide to me a piece of my rowing puzzle.

I would meet Dave Harmon on the proverbial field of combat, at the 1976 Women's Nationals. His New England prep school eight surprised my defending national champion high school crew from San Diego. Creamed us off the line, straining like my picture of his Super Boat.

My team would have to settle for winning the junior single, double, quad and four, the novice eight (against all the colleges) and both wherries. And receive an invitation to the Olympic Women's Double Trials. *Quel désastre!*

But enough of looking into the future!

* * * * *

In 1972, I know the Super Boat only by reputation, a reputation as Gods!

So the anticipated coming of Super Boat *Coach* Steve Gladstone takes on messianic overtones at the 1972 Lightweight Selection Camp.

A day or two after he arrives, Steve takes me aside and asks me to switch to port as a favor to him, so that I can stroke the eight. Just like that.

"Pete, would you be so kind as to switch to port, so that you can stroke the eight for me?"

Oh . . . my . . . God!

My heart is in my throat. All those years are about to pay off.

Life is indeed good!

Mais, bien sûr.

"Seat racing," a sort of Darwinism in boats, seat racing begins.

Two cox fours, side-by-side, race a specific distance and carefully note the result.

Then a guy in one boat exchanges seats with a guy in the other boat. The boats race again and carefully note the resulting change.

It's pretty simple. Speed up the boat you move into, and you win the seat race, you beat the man you exchanged with.

Over a period of time, it is fairly a straightforward matter to identify the eight best guys. The rest are extinct: Australopithecines, Neanderthals.

Dodos.

As the heir-apparent, I stroke one of the fours involved. It is my *H.M.S. Beagle*, and for several days I am not switched. No need. Steve is concentrating on selecting those who will sit behind me in the National Eight.

Life is very good!

The boat is nearly set when Steve switches me, on a whim, just to be fair. I lose big. I get blown out.

Blown out of the water.

I'm shocked. Steve is shocked. Everyone is shocked. No one has an explanation.

All of a sudden Steve's golden boy is exposed. Five years have changed nothing, and Fred Leonard's judgment is confirmed! Just like my senior year at Penn, I'm not a boat *mover*. I'm an anchor, a boat *stopper!*

I'm a dodo.

In short order I am seat raced off the port side, switched to starboard, seat raced off the starboard side. My life is in ruins.

The Ides of March.

Steve?

> *"Et tu Brute?"*
> - Julius Caesar

Now Steve Gladstone and I go way back. Knew him when he was still "Happyrocks." I'd bunked on his hallway at Kent in 1960, the year he was Captain of the Crew.

The year he was Zeus!

He is a father figure of sorts to me. I think of this man, and a tear comes to my eye.

I would do anything for this Steve Gladstone, my idol since prep school. And I know he would do anything for me.

So I ask Steve what I am doing wrong.

"Give me a clue, Steve. It's certainly not strength, not fitness, not experience, not poise . . . but it *must* be something."

Steve is terribly embarrassed. There is nothing he can say. He doesn't have a clue.

After all, we *all* start clueless.

Deja vu for me.
Curse of the JV Scar all over again.

* * * * *

That year the National Eight was spared the inclusion of an athlete who wasn't moving boats, namely me, but I was replaced by a man named Pete Billings, a man apparently less well-qualified in all the tangible criteria I respected: ergometer, strength, stairs, talent, maturity, fitness, experience, tactics.

I had it all . . . all except the ability to move boats.

Oh. Did I mention yet that the eight we are putting together will tour Europe undefeated with Pete Billings *very* capably handling the stroke seat? Did I mention that?

There's got to be a reason. Just *has* to be!

That seat race defeat kept me on a path that lasted fifteen more years. I had to know what I was doing wrong. I had to solve the riddle. There would be no peace until I understood.

The next time you call Composite Engineering, tell Pete I said hello. Yes, Pete Billings is still contributing to our sport.

Still moving boats . . . excuse the pun.

Peter's Island

So what happens to me after being bounced out of the National Eight? Fairthy begs me to be the single sculler in Europe, and, fool that I am, I agree.

I have about a week to get my head together and prepare for the Nationals in the single. And I have my own brand-new *Stämpfli* single, my pride and joy, the best boat made anywhere in the world, the *Ferrari* of racing shells, arrived that very spring by plane from Zurich, now sporting a basketball scar on its starboard rigger.

I resolve to enter the quarter-mile dash as well as the regular 2,000-meter race. Under the circumstances, I expect to have trouble making the finals in "the distance" but hope I have retained my potency from the previous year in the dash. If I at least medal in the dash I can hold my head high with my teammates in Europe.

But I am still pretty shaken by my seat race experience, and I will need a bit of luck to find again my sculling rhythm.

Not a good idea . . . for me, or for anyone else I've ever known, to depend on luck in a sporting contest.

I presume you've heard of Murphy's Law. You know, whatever can go wrong will go wrong?

Very powerful in my life. How 'bout yours?

It's my experience that Murphy's Law seems to be directly proportional to the importance of the situation. The more that's at stake, the more inevitable the disaster.

So here's how the Nationals went for me in 1972:

* * * * *

By the time I arrive at the regatta site on my home Schuylkill River course in Philadelphia I'm going reasonably well again in my single, but nowhere near my best, and my head is still completely up my ass.

My heat in the dash is a breeze, literally. It's windy, but I qualify without sweat.

The distance is another matter. There are a couple of guys really flying this year, Bill Belden from Undine, of course, who beat me in the dash in 1971, and Dr. Larry Klekatsky, an emergency room physician from New York Athletic Club.

My heat reads like a N.Y.A.C. team practice. Is this seat taken?
Larry's in there, as is the defending national champion, for Heaven's sake, a guy named Jon Sonberg who wears mirror aviator shades all the time, like the Southern cop in *Cannonball Run*, as well as some high school kid who is already being touted as the next great lightweight sensation. I have to beat at least one of them, since only three will qualify for the final.
Oh my!

As I settle into the body of the race, Klekatsky's gone on the field. I am in fourth, closely following the other two N.Y.A.C. guys. Under the Strawberry Mansion Bridge, the high school kid fades. Then we slip past the Canoe Club, and I slip past Sonberg into second. Very satisfying. By the end of the race there is more jockeying behind me, and the defending champion ends up not qualifying, mirror shades and all.
So there!

For me the final is an anticlimax. Belden and Klekatsky have a monumental battle, and I slink over the finish line unnoticed about twenty seconds later in fifth.
Not bad, considering.
Best I could do that day, but meanwhile my teammates in our National Lightweight Eight, with me now excised, surgically removed, win by lengths and lengths of open water.

Oceans and oceans.

I turn my attention to the dash final. I remind myself how good I am in this most pure, most exquisite of events.
I remind myself that just twelve months earlier I was my country's fastest lightweight dashman, and only defeated *myself* with a crab.
This year is going to be *my* year!
Trouble is the weather is unsettled. It's windy from the west during the heats, and I've never been all that confident in crosswinds. It's tough to settle . . . *settle* to a 44 if the water's not mirror-smooth.

I could use a little luck. I pray for flat water the next day . . . or at least a sheltered lane.

Murphy's Law alert! Murphy's Law alert!

I'm worried. I know the last quarter mile in Philadelphia like the back of my hand. In the morning, the water is most often calm. But in the afternoon in July, it's a crap shoot. With a crosswind from the west, Peter's Island shelters Lanes Four, Five and Six for the first thirty-five strokes, and leaves the other lanes screwed!

God, I hate to have my fate depend on a lane draw.

And Peter's Island. It has rarely been kind to me. Scene of Al Campbell's crab.

And once I almost died rowing beside Peter's Island . . .

* * * * *

It's a bitter-cold midwinter morning just half a year earlier, and I am all alone in my single rowing upstream at my anaerobic threshold, death from hypothermia lurking just inches away, just below the surface I glide over. My starboard blade is less than three feet from the vertical west wall of Peter's Island.

Unbeknownst to me as I blast along, relying on my meticulous memory of the river to allow me to navigate without ever looking around, I am sneaking up on and scaring the Hell out of an indolent Canada Goose, a goose too lazy to fly south for the winter, a goose now a formidable obstacle floating in my path.

My bow ball gooses the goose, leaving its rather ample body careening between my quickly advancing hull and the Peter's Island wall.

The goose panics.

I hear splashing, beating wings . . . very close.

Suddenly, WHAP!

The twenty-pound goose fuselage hits me full tilt in the side of the head. All its other paths of retreat having been cut off by Peter's Island, the bird has flown straight into me and nearly knocked me out cold.

Somehow I hang onto consciousness and live long enough to learn that six months later I have indeed drawn an unprotected Lane Two in my 1972 U.S. Championship Quarter-Mile Dash final.

* * * * *

Now the six lanes on an official rowing course are numbered with Lane One on the side of the course where the officials stand. In Philadelphia, Lane One is next to the officials on the river's eastern bank and Lane Six is all the way over in the middle of the river next to Peter's Island.

The island is long and thin, covered with trees, and stretches from the quarter-mile-to-go post all the way to about 150 meters to go on the race course. For its entire length, the boat in Lane Six rows only a very few feet from the vertical bank of Peter's Island, and in a western crosswind Lane Six is completely sheltered.

Not so for *my* Lane Two. Oh no!

No shelter. None. And as we line up for the dash final, there's a crosswind from the west.

Big one.

Of course! Murphy's Law!

The start commands come in French, in honor of the fact that the first international regatta was held at the 1900 Olympics in Paris.

Êtes vous prêt? (No, I'm not ready. No, but thanks for asking. Can we talk about this? Can we put this off for a week? Or a year?) *Partez!*

Dr. Larry Klekatsky, a true sportsman all the time but a lucky son of a bitch at this particular moment, is in the smooth, sheltered water of Lane Six, and of course he's gone, just like he was in my distance heat.

Some new guy named Ted Van Dusen, rowing in a boat, get this, a boat he built *himself* in his basement, he's taking full advantage of Lane Five, and has me by a length. I'm floundering and feeling sorry for myself, but somehow I'm ahead of everybody else.

Bill Belden, my respected friend and worthy adversary, who beat me by two feet just last year, at least he's in Lane One, and even worse off than me.

Perhaps there *is* justice!

End of the island. No more shelter for anybody. Now at least we're *all* floundering! Twenty strokes to go. Let's get this over with. I've got to go give myself a swirly and then get on a plane for Europe and drive around all my teammates who know what a boat stopper I have turned out to be.

Wonder if everybody else is . . . Hey! What's got into Bill Belden?

Bill Belden bursts by me. He's caught Ted! Can you believe it? He's even caught Larry!

Bravo Bill! You probably remember your 1974 world lightweight singles title.

Me, I remember your 1972 dash. Belden's Law must be: To Hell with Murphy's Law!

Good for you!

Ta Da

I go to Europe, no closer to an answer as to how to move boats, and return to a new milepost in my life journey. My latest freshman team contains my first boat stopper, big, strong, committed . . . and slow. As I write this book, I have his name in my daily journal on a shelf somewhere, but I don't dare look him up. I'm too embarrassed, for now it is I who have to mouth the words that once came from the mouth of Fred Leonard, that just last summer came from the mouth of Steve Gladstone.

At the end of this, my third season of coaching, my squad enters the Eastern Sprints undefeated and rowing in a German Karlisch shell so hard to balance that the varsity and JVs had shunned it for almost five years. Getting it ready to race has taught me a great deal about rigging, and my guys love the boat.

photo credit: Peter Mallory

1973 Penn Freshman Lightweights, Undefeated Regular Season:
cox'n Galen Rogers, Ron Hendrickson, Sam Lamar, Brian Keane, Glenn Simon,
Mark Davison, Dave Farwell, Don Cooper, Pete Holding.

We win our heat with Galen Rogers, the first female cox'n in U.S. history ever to compete in a male championship rowing event.

Ta Da!

As I recall she earned that distinction by about fifteen minutes, the advantage of rowing in the first heat of the first event on the first day of the first major championship of the year, but precedent is precedent, and I remain very proud. I bask in her reflected glory.

She became a doctor. She's practicing in Heaven now.

Clouds threatening all day. Finals in the afternoon.
Five minutes before and five minutes after the freshman lightweight final the winds are dead calm. Dead calm! *During* our freshman lightweight final a line squall brings thirty-mile-an-hour gusts and crashing waves.
From the first stroke we flounder in the Karlisch. A relatively unremarkable crew from Harvard, in a stable, reliable American Pocock racing shell, holds us even for 500, takes two seats on our crab by the 1,000, breaks it open to three-quarters of a length on a Hellish second crab in the third 500, and we collapse, badly beaten to the finish.

* * * * *

Hera, vengeful goddess, d*efinitely* must have it in for me, don't you think?
You've got to admit! I really have had more than my fair share of bad fortune, and much of it weather-related, as I think back . . .
Hmm!

* * * * *

I return to Philadelphia with my third consecutive Eastern Sprints second place crew, with a heavy heart and a plan to seek a new coaching opportunity somewhere, anywhere on the West Coast.

> *"Go west, young man!"*
> - John Babsone Lane Soule,
> *Terre Haute Express*

* * * * *

With the benefit of hindsight, I can report to you that this last effort of mine as Freshman Lightweight Coach for the University of Pennsylvania will bear abundant fruit just three years later. As seniors, my guys will win the Sprints and go to Henley.

Wish I could have foreseen what the future holds as I make my way back to Philadelphia this spring.

Might have cheered me up a bit.

Afterlife

The days after the 1973 Eastern Sprints find me again unstuck in time, preparing to load my *Stämpfli* single onto my little red Fiat *Ottocinquanta* and head west to seek my fortune.

On one of those indescribable early June days in Philadelphia I sit outside the boathouse and stare across the river. The sun has regained its summer strength, and the pungent smell of blooming flowers dulls my senses. Trees hang heavy with new foliage, which rustle in the gentle breeze. The Schuylkill River oozes past Boathouse Row, and bugs buzz in lazy circles.

It's beautiful, but today I hardly notice, way too busy feeling sorry for myself. The first year I coached we lost two races in the season. The second year only one. This year we have been undefeated . . . and yet we have come in second at the Sprints for a third year in a row. In a squall. How could such a thing happen? I am overwhelmed by missed opportunities.

Practice has been over for more than a week. My kids have gone home for the summer, and I am alone . . . sitting on a bench at the boathouse overlooking the docks, feeling as empty as the locker rooms upstairs.

Some old guy walks by me, stops and stares out across the river.

Never seen him before. Businessman, distinguished, a touch of class in his stature. If I'm not mistaken, he's probably in his forties, maybe six feet tall, maybe 170. I don't know.

He smiles . . .

I'm barely aware that he's talking to me.

Obviously a stranger . . . doesn't know anybody in town . . . came down to the river on a whim . . . must have been an oarsman once a very long time ago . . . not a Penn man, though . . . not a fellow Quaker . . . but did he mention he once rowed out of this very boathouse?

Interesting . . .

Not really.

I'm too busy rerowing my life, rubbing my JV Scar like Lady Macbeth.

Wait a minute!
Did he just say he wished he could go out for a row?
In a pair?
With me?
Does he think I'm out of my fugging mind?
Come on! I wasn't born yesterday! Rowing in a good boat really is better than sex! But rowing in a bad boat is . . . well . . .
. . . and a pair worst of all!
The most unforgiving of all boats.

Not a "double," two guys with two sculling oars each, easy, elegant, symmetrical. In French, *deux en couple*. As in "coop-le." Even sounds nice. I imagine Catherine Deneuve cooing in my ear, *"Voulez-vous ramer deux en couple avec moi, ce soir?"*
"Avec Moi? Mais bien sûr!"
No. Not a double. No Catherine Deneuve. *C'est domage.*
A "pair," two guys with one big clunky sweep oar each, ungainly, the port rower in front of the starboard rower, asymmetrical, retarded.
I imagine Madame Defarge looking up from her knitting, spitting tobacco juice on the cobbles, pointing at me and passing judgment: *"Deux en pointe!"*
She puts all her derision onto the final "t" sound, and it grates my ear as I am led to the tumbrels.

A pair.
God-awful hard boat to steer, to balance, to row.
God-awful.

If I end up in Hell, which seems a perfectly reasonable presumption on this particular day, I fully expect to be directed to the bulletin board at the River Styx Boathouse, and if I am *very* fortunate, I will be sent to the tanks, the still-water tanks, or I'll be chained to a noisy rowing machine with a handle made of broken glass and the guy from Ben Hur screaming and cracking his whip at me for the next thousand years.
That is, if I am *very* fortunate . . .

If I'm not . . . I'll be assigned to row a pair with a total stranger.

Simple as that.

All this flashes through my mind as this lonely man with a kind face smiles down at me and suggests we go rowing . . . in a pair.
Him and me!
Him . . . and me . . .
What the Hell . . .

Literally.

Now wouldn't this be the perfectly appropriate end to a perfectly horrible day in the midst of a perfectly horrible year?
I *deserve* this!
My mouth forms the words of acceptance as I listen, detached, from somewhere across the river.
I'm having another **OUT**-of-boat experience.

His name is Dewey Something or other.
What the Hell kind of first name is Dewey, anyway? We shake hands. I find Dewey some *really* dirty clothes in the lost-and-found box.
We pick out a couple of oars from the rack. Get this. He has never rowed with modern shovel blades.
Why am I not surprised?
We pick a pair-oared shell off the rack, set it in the water, step in and push away from the dock.
Just like that.

As we sit and tie in, Dewey asks me what style I row. I look back over my shoulder and smugly tell him I can do them all: American, Russian, East German, West German, accelerated slide, steady slide, decelerated slide, explosive power, steady power, one hand, two hands, fast hands, slow hands, gradual roll, snap roll, no pause, pause at the catch, pause at the finish. I can do them ALL!
I'm absolutely insufferable . . .

Nevertheless, soon we are gliding upriver deep in conversation and actually *doing* all those styles.
And having fun.

You know, the boat feels okay for having some old fart in the bow seat and my sorry ass at stroke. Soon we are three miles and more up the river.

We discover we actually have something in common. He tells me he went to Stanford, and Jimmy Beggs was his coach. Gentleman Jim Beggs! *My* freshman coach.

Is this a small world or what?

We swap affectionate stories. I never knew Jimmy coached at Stanford.

I'm starting to figure out this Dewey guy is okay after all. The boat is flying, and I've never enjoyed myself so much. Imagine that!

We are just about back to the dock when he lets slip that he once actually rowed a pair with Jimmy Beggs as his cox'n.

(Yes, pairs come with and without cox'ns, just like fours.)

So I guess that explains why our pair is going as well as it is.

This guy has a little bit of experience . . .

All right, I have to admit it. This has been downright wonderful. This is the best pair I have ever rowed in! Maybe the best boat I ever rowed in . . .

Can you imagine?

Deux en pointe . . .

Wait a minute!

Where did you say you and Jim rowed your cox pair? Helsinki? As in 1952 Olympics Helsinki, Finland Helsinki?

Holy cow! I'm rowing with an Olympian!

Too soon we are back at the dock. Dewey is aglow. Magical afternoon. Can he buy me dinner? You bet he can! I want to hear more about Helsinki. I suggest Schnockey's Seafood House, a Philadelphia tradition.

There we are in a booth sharing a huge pot of steamers, and Dewey continues the story. Seems his boat was off the pace at the Olympics, but he and his partner, I never caught the other guy's name, came away believing that they might actually have what it took to be competitive the next time.

My ears perk up.

"The next time?" I ask.

The *next* time?

Dewey continues.

Trouble was Jim Beggs had to get back to grad school or something, so Dewey and the other guy put off their own careers and embarked on a four-year Olympic odyssey, this time in a pair without cox'n, spending their last year coincidentally rowing out of the Penn Boathouse.

"What happened?" I ask. They went to Melbourne in 1956 . . .

. . . and they won.

They *won?* The Olympics?

I have just spent the afternoon rowing a straight pair with an Olympic straight pair champion? I nearly faint.

I imagine dying . . . and somehow I'm going to Heaven after all. I go the bulletin board at the boathouse. Sy Cromwell has put in a good word for me, and I am assigned to row a pair with Duvall Hecht.

Afterlife is *good!*

Weejuns

I leave Philadelphia for parts west a few days later, and the last person I see before jumping into my car is Joan Lind from Long Beach Rowing Association. I had developed a mad crush on her from afar the previous summer in Europe when she was in the U.S. women's double and I was the lightweight single. She's in town for the Women's Nationals.

I say, "Hi, goodbye."

The first stop on my trip to find my fortune is the Intercollegiate Rowing Association Championships in Syracuse to speak to UCLA Coach Jerry Johnson. He was the first to encourage me to move to California.

He breaks the news that there will be no place for me at UCLA but suggests I head for Long Beach.

"Okay."

On the road I think of Heaven and Joan Lind and Olympic pairs and Jim Moroney.

* * * * *

Jim Moroney.

That year Jim had been a sophomore at Penn, a fellow Quaker, and a past graduate of St. Joe's Prep in Philadelphia, with an extra emphasis on prep, as in Bass Weejuns, no socks, LaCoste shirts, inside out, collar up, with an incandescent smile that could light up a room.

And what a rower!

We became good friends a year earlier when he was pledging my old fraternity, Kappa Sigma, which had become a bit of an animal house since I had graduated.

"Jim, we're brothers! A.E.K.D.B."

(That's secret fraternity talk. If I told you what it meant, I'd have to kill you.)

Jack Barclackey, Jim's freshman heavyweight coach and an old teammate of mine at Undine, is terrified that someone might accidentally injure Jim during the upcoming Hell Night festivities. Years ago I'd missed my own Hell Night. Got the haircut (remember the photo?), then took off for Cornell for my oh-so-memorable first collegiate crew race.

I eagerly volunteer to be Jim's bodyguard. Complete a circle of sorts.

And so as Jim wends his way, blindfolded, through the maze of mostly imaginary tortures a Kappa Sig pledge must endure on this final night before becoming a brother, I fend off various awkward advances from inebriated upperclassmen. Jim survives unscathed.

Jack and I celebrate.

Prematurely, it turns out.

The next day, during the formal, solemn induction ceremony, everyone in suits and ties, someone breaks Jim's collarbone.

Don't even ask.

A.E.K.D.B., my ass!

We are at the beginning of the collegiate season, and there are less than two months until the 1972 Olympic Trials . . .

Fortunately there's a happy ending to this story. Turns out you can row while your collarbone heals (a trick I rediscovered years later after a velodrome accident). Jim's Penn boat wins the IRAs . . . and Jim makes the Olympic Team rowing in the Vesper coxless four in Munich.

Bravo Jim!

And a standing "boovation" for Kappa Sig!

After Jim returns from Germany, we sit down and talk technique till midnight. Turns out his boat: Jim, Bill Miller, Chuck Hewitt, my friend from the Harvard Lightweight Super Boat (!) and Dick Dreissigacker (Go buy an oar or an erg from Dick, cofounder of Concept II!), and their expatriate German coach, Dietrich Rose, had spent countless hours analyzing films of East German boats, the best in the world in those times.

Their conclusion? The East Germans row high and fast . . . but not as "hard" as most American crews, their boats accelerating smoothly from catch to finish, no wasted effort, no visible strain, no sign of explosiveness.

Almost a sculler's sensitivity.

Hmm!

Jim describes to me how the Vesper four would concentrate on keeping the boat flowing forward quickly with the minimum effort possible, during both training and racing. To Jim it almost felt like three-quarter power at the catch!

Reminds me of Arthur Lydiard's approach to running.

Hmm!

And that Vesper boat easily won the Olympic Trials over much more experienced and aggressive boats!

* * * * *

And so it is Jim Moroney's enigmatic words that echo in my head as I drive cross-country into the unknown.

Five days later, on a sparkling Southern California afternoon, I pull into the parking lot at Long Beach, and within three hours, three short hours, head coach Ed Graham has hired me to coach the state university's lightweight crew and given me a room at his house to sleep in.

I am even invited to row my single in the following morning's Long Beach Rowing Association practice alongside the best scullers in the country, including Joan Lind, just back from Philadelphia, having won the U.S. singles championship and having qualified to represent the U.S. at the 1973 Worlds in the single . . .

. . . and she's surprised as the dickens to see me again so soon.

Pinch me.

Call Me Ishmael

Wonderful news!

There is to be an exhibition lightweight eight event at the 1973 World Championships in Moscow!

And, after his Herculean efforts organizing the 1972 U.S. Team Tour of Europe, my good friend F. Fairthington Farthington has been appointed the National Lightweight Men's Coach!

So after a couple of weeks settling into my new home in Long Beach, I bid my new friends farewell and return to the East Coast to assume my role as Fairthy's National Assistant Coach.

My destruction in seat racing the previous year has convinced me that if I ever want to achieve greatness, it will have to be as a coach rather than as rower, and here I am already on the U.S. staff and going to my first World Championships!

Fairthy Farthington will be my Captain Ahab, and I and the crew we assemble will follow this man to the other side of the world in search of our destiny.

Life is good.

Selection camp will take place at Dartmouth immediately after the Men's Nationals in Camden, New Jersey. The first problem is that there are too many athletes who want to attend. We have to cull out the herd down to fewer than twenty athletes. Slyly I suggest we invite anybody who had just won a national championship and test the rest on the Penn ergometers in nearby Philadelphia.

Fairthy agrees.

"Make it so."
- Jean Luc Picard

What Fairthy doesn't realize, and I of course do, is that Mark Davison, the best guy on my freshman crew from that very spring, undefeated until that line squall, destined to go to Henley three years hence, has just been part of Fred Leonard's national champion intermediate heavyweight cox four, so he is a national champion, so he gets invited, and Fairthy only finds out he's been invited when we all assemble a couple of days and a couple hundred miles later on the dock at Dartmouth.

Fairthy is not amused. To his mind, a freshman with only one year of experience under his belt does not have the seasoning suitable for inclusion in a national team effort. Surely we left behind in Philadelphia many athletes more deserving! Too late to do anything about Mark, but my own reputation with Fairthy is fast eroding.

Seat racing begins immediately, two sessions a day for a week. Time constraints prevent every individual from actually getting a shot on the water at every other. Even in two weeks a selection camp coach has little time to spend distinguishing between seventh and eighth and ninth on the ladder for the port side or the starboard side, and little interest in distinguishing between first and second. What counts is *the boundary* on each side: who is third and fourth (and makes the boat) and who is fifth and sixth (and doesn't), and so Fairthy quickly focuses his attention on just a few rowers.

Trouble is F. Fairthington Farthington is all too human. He arrives at the camp with his mind made up about just about everybody. And why not? Enough guys to make a great eight are already well known to him. They have already proven their excellence in collegiate rowing and during the previous year's European tour!

All that is required is confirmation, coronation.

* * * * *

As I now think back to that selection camp from the perspective of middle age, I think of two guys who ended up on that Dartmouth dock that first day never having met before, and, as far as I know, never meeting again. The first is my friend, Penn freshman Mark Davison, 6'4" with flame red hair, sensational erg, great natural athlete, great competitor, with a great future ahead of him. The second guy is my 1972 teammate on the European tour, former Princeton captain Pete Maxon, 6'3" with flame red hair, sensational erg, great natural athlete, great competitor, with a great past behind him.

Hmm!

Similar . . . yet so different. Pete's confident, competent, fully muscled, incredibly aggressive, a real head shaker and oar bender, already a collegiate champion, a Royal Henley champion, a member of Pete Billings' undefeated eight last year, a true role model and, not incidentally, the *protégé* of his varsity coach at Princeton, none other than F. Fairthington Farthington.

Mark's strong, but he's a stylist, and nobody's heard of him. Nothing to hear.

Not yet, anyway.

* * * * *

With all the experienced talent at the camp, Fairthy has no intention of sending a first-year rower to do battle at the Worlds. Sure that's prejudice, but isn't that also sound judgment?

So, to eliminate Mark from consideration right off the bat, and perhaps to pimp me, Fairthy seat races Mark against one of the several Harvard boys present, an English major, a friend of Fairthy's, a stud.

Trouble is Mark wins. Wins big.

Must be some mistake, right? Try it again against another favorite. Mark wins again.

Horizon job.

There's only one thing to do, right? Open your mind? Change your preconceptions, right?

Wrong. Fairthy keeps looking and finally finds someone to beat Mark: a kid from Frostbite Falls, Minnesota named Eric Aserlind.

Rowed heavyweight for Wisconsin. But who's ever heard of *him?* Not an Ivy bone in his body. He's a cheese-head, a Badger, for Heaven's sake! Can't be very good, right? No rowing worthy of notice between the Appalachians and the Rockies.

So Fairthy has his excuse. Mark is set aside and never seat raced again. Out of the boat.

Eric, too. He has served his purpose.

Isn't life grand?

How about Pete? Pete loses big his first seat race.

Open water big.

And his second.

Disneyland big.

And so he, too, is never seat raced again. He's in the boat.

HE'S IN THE BOAT!

Pete Mallory's Disease

At the end of the week the boatings are announced, Pete in the six seat of the National Eight going to the Worlds, Mark and Eric in the National "JV" that would race in Canada. The two boats hit the water and guess what?

Right. I've already told you what JVs do to Varsities. This JV kicks the National Eight's ass. Three times over 1,000 meters, the margin never less than two lengths of open water. A joke.

But nobody's laughing.

At least there is justice on the water. The rejected seat racing results are vindicated.

But as I watch from the launch, I am as astonished as everybody else. How could the first boat be *so* slow? Jim Moroney comes back to me. Pete Maxon, with his explosive catch that shakes the entire boat, is the antithesis of what Jim had described as good rowing.

But I know the technique well. It's the way Fred Leonard had taught me to row. As far as I know it is the way everybody's supposed to row.

Pete Maxon is my ideal, my hero. Nobody does it better than Pete Maxon.

A thought forms in my mind. Could this be why I lost my seat race last year? Is Pete Maxon displaying the classic symptoms of Pete Mallory's Disease?

* * * * *

I think back to my own brutal 1972 summer. We were halfway through our European tour, and I had been getting my ass kicked all over the place in my lightweight single. There must have been seven or eight guys faster than me in Europe, and at every finish line I felt like telling all my competitors how lucky they were that Bill Belden or Larry Klekatsky wasn't there to show them how fast an American could really be.

When we got to Klagenfurt, Austria, I took a week off from my single when teammate Chuck Crawford, a fellow Philadelphian and

Rutgers grad with a charitable soul, offered to row a lightweight double with me. One day, as we practiced out on the *Worthersee*, I asked Chuck if he had any idea why I had lost all my seat races.

I'll never forget what he said.

He told me you could tell whenever I moved into a boat.

"We could tell whenever you moved into a boat, Peter. We could really feel your explosive leg drive. There was no question you were one of the strongest guys on the team . . .

"Just like Pete Maxon."

* * * * *

Chuck Crawford was paying me a compliment in Klagenfurt, but years earlier another teammate had also commented on my thunderous drive . . . and he didn't mean it as a compliment.

His name was Bill Wark. He rowed behind me in the bow seat of that Undine eight that played "Bash the Buoys" with Detroit at Orchard Beach in 1965. 'Bout my size, short haircut, glasses like Fairthy's, quiet on a team of show-offs.

I had never met him before that summer, and I think I rowed with him in a double exactly once in early June. Barely knew his name when I read it on the bulletin board: Bill in bow, me in stroke.

In 1965 Undine was a team of good double scullers, led by Manno and Walsh, former schoolboy national champions, and there was a lot of jockeying for position every day in practice. Don Callahan and I had been rowing together for a couple of weeks, and we were usually second fastest . . . but this day Bill Wark and I couldn't keep up with *anybody*.

I assumed it was Bill's fault. Couldn't be me! I was a stud! (The Curse of the JV Scar still lay nearly two years in the future.)

Suddenly Bill exclaims, "Now I know what's wrong! No wonder the boat's going so bad! You're exploding your legs at the catch!"

As if that was something *bad* . . .

I explode back, "I have been working my ass off for a year on leg explosion in my collegiate eight, and there was no way I'm going, to all of a sudden, change just for you!

"So there!"

* * * * *

I cringe just thinking of it now.

Luckily for Bill, he never had to row in a double with me again after that terrible day. Unluckily for me, as it turned out, for I missed the chance to learn an important lesson from Bill Wark.

Curvature of the Earth

Years later, in the launch at the National Team Camp in Dartmouth, I think again about how Chuck had described my seat racing. Images race by in my mind.

What if my explosiveness disrupted everyone else's flow, disrupted the boat's flow? Could a boat really travel down the course through water with explosive power?

Couldn't there possibly be a better way?

As I sit here at this camp, in this launch, I really don't know, but it is food for thought as I ponder how Pete Maxon could possibly lose a seat race to anyone on Earth.

Bill Wark.

Bill Wark . . .   Something else in the back of my mind.

Now that I think of it, there's another guy at camp in Dartmouth who has me recalling my day in a double with Bill Wark, and, interestingly enough, this other guy is also getting the Mark Davison treatment from Fairthy. He's my old teammate and friend Larry Wittig. We had been coaching side-by-side on the Schuylkill for a couple of years, and I left for California comforted by the knowledge that he would replace me as Fred Leonard's Freshman Lightweight Coach.

Larry is like Bill Wark . . . and he isn't. Whereas Bill had been quiet and polite, Larry is quite simply the grossest guy I have ever met. But, like Bill, Larry is smooth as silk on the water. He is also the lightest athlete at camp, hardly more than 140 amongst a bunch of solid 170 pounders.

First-generation ergometers are massive machines, and the big guns like Pete and Mick Feld make them groan and clang like a cracked Liberty Bell. Larry gets on, and there is *dead silence*.

I kid you not!

You have to look twice to realize he is even rowing . . . and getting a good score at that.

Hmm!

But to F. Fairthington Farthington, Chaucer scholar, University of Pennsylvania Class of 1963, St. Elmo's Club, or was it St. Anthony's Hall? I forget. It was one of the two of them. Anyway, to F. Fairthington Farthington, little Larry Wittig, Drech Tech Class of '72, from the tiny coal-mining town of Tamaqua in Northeastern Pennsylvania, he might as well be Pete Mallory to John Hartigan.

He's completely invisible.

I can't help wondering if things might be different had Larry been a proper graduate of the Ancient Eight, an English major who quoted great books and didn't integrate into normal conversation quite so many slang terms for female pudenda.

Larry Wittig, who lives his life in a manner Geoffrey Chaucer would have understood and appreciated, Larry never loses a seat race at the National Camp . . . not a single one . . . and, like Mark Davison and Eric Aserlind and the two guys who came all the way from UCLA and a whole host of others, Larry is never, ever even considered for the National Eight.

Interesting.

Especially interesting now that Larry is stroking the other rejects, and they are crushing the National Eight none of them could make.

I am in the launch, watching it all and having another **OUT**-of-boat experience . . . thinking of Bill Wark, concluding I probably should have listened better that day in the double.

* * * * *

A couple of years ago I visited Bill in Washington, D.C. . . . . at the Vietnam Memorial Wall.

> *"Though I've belted you and flayed you,*
> *By the livin' Gawd that made you,*
> *You're a better man than I am, Gunga Din!"*
> \- Rudyard Kipling

106

photo credit: Peter Mallory

Bill Wark, waiting to weigh in at the Nationals in 1965.

"Rest in peace, Bill Wark.

"You made the ultimate sacrifice for our country in the war I avoided, and so I never got the chance to tell you in person how much I respect the way you rowed boats and lived your life and how it took me twenty years to finally appreciate how right you had been about boat moving that day back in 1965."

Get Rid of the Redhead

Back to the tragedy at hand. F. Fairthington Farthington has a problem. His golden boat is double-butt slow.

Luckily for him, the heavyweight selection camp is also being held at Dartmouth in 1973, and many of the best coaches in America are rolling through town to see how things are going.

To his credit, Fairthy asks one coach after another for advice. I am invisible in the launch and listen. Every single one he asks starts with the words "Get rid of the redhead . . ." followed by one suggestion or another, and ending with " . . . get rid of the redhead."

Each time Fairthy gets the advice to remove Maxon, he seeks out someone else, soon *anyone* else. I imagine he is trying to finally find someone who actually likes the way Pete rows.

He never does.

Never.

After three days of this he sets the final boatings. Fairthy announces to the entire squad assembled on the dock that he has sought out and accepted the advice of all the great minds of American rowing, and though, of course, they haven't told him anything he didn't already know (gag!), their collective wisdom has allowed him to come to the right conclusion a little more quickly.

Drum roll. The envelope, please . . .

Pete is moved from the six seat to the four seat in the first boat. Larry Wittig and Mark Davison and Eric Aserlind remain in the JV.

* * * * *

I must breathe again. Twenty-seven years later I am turning blue.

* * * * *

We shove off. The JV kicks the National Eight's ass one last time. Three lengths.

Curvature of the Earth.

I secretly rejoice and mourn in a single burst of stomach bile.

From that day forward, I am assigned to coach a very understandably disillusioned JV and sent downstream of the Dartmouth dock while the national boat practices alone upstream.

Simple solution to a complex problem, don't you think?

The JV wins easily the Canadian Henley. The National Eight comes in last at the Worlds.

And they have trouble making weight there, too. In fact, several end up in the hospital in Moscow.

* * * * *

Hmm!

Perhaps they could have used a guy, like Larry for instance, who would not only have made them faster but also made weight for the entire boat!

I can't help but believe that eight legitimate seat race winners, Larry and Eric and perhaps Mark included, would today be esteemed and respected as 1973 world champions if only they had been given the opportunity they deserved and earned.

Think about it. That JV was the fastest lightweight eight on the face of the Earth that year! Would have won the Worlds just as they were boated.

So there!

Some of the guys from this ill-fated camp rowed again in 1974, and the U.S. *did* win the Worlds, Eric the Cheese-Head (Who'd a thunk it?) among them. Congratulations! Good for them all!

Proves it could have been done, nay, *should* have been done, in 1973!

But not Mark Davison, or Larry Wittig, or Pete Maxon, tragic heroes all. Nineteen seventy-three turns out to be their last chance, their only chance. Isn't life grand?

And not Fairthy Farthington, either, to my mind the greatest tragedy of all, for it was his vision that had inspired a whole country. From East Coast and West Coast and points in between they had come because of him. They were arrows in his quiver, and he should have been the world champion coach.

After all, despite his best efforts, the best eight in the world had been assembled at his camp! He just didn't recognize them.

I thought I knew Fairthy well . . .

. . . but he was blind to what he had in front of him.

But this was not entirely his fault!

His sport denied him the eyes with which to see the true talent arrayed before him. His sport denied him the tools to open his mind past explosive catches, past the Ivy League, to appreciate Mark Davison and Eric Aserlind, to tolerate Larry Wittig, to help Pete Maxon.

But with all its conventional wisdom and closed-mindedness, it is our sport that I blame!

F. Fairthington Farthington could have been a great man.

Was I the only one who noticed this tragedy?
So it goes . . .

And I still believe Pete Maxon is one of the most magnificent rowers I have ever seen. I wish we could all replay that year and get it right this time.

Time Machine

If I had a time machine, I would go back to 1973 and take Pete Maxon aside and teach him how to move boats.

Yes, now I know how to move boats . . . and now I know how to teach it.

So I'd teach Pete. I would do everything in my power to include this larger-than-life athlete in this larger-than-life effort to boat the best lightweight eight the world had yet seen.

And while I was at it, I would travel *at least* one additional year into the past and teach myself how to move boats, too, so I could hang onto my own seat in the 1972 eight. For my performance was not all that different from Pete's in 1973. I couldn't move boats, just like Pete.
It's just that *my* seat race results were acted upon.

Absent a time machine, as Assistant National Coach I was scheduled to accompany Fairthy and his newly selected *"trente-six fois merde"* U.S. Eight to the Worlds in Moscow that summer, but Fairthy hadn't spoken a word to me since I had first pointed out to him in private that he was ignoring his own seat race results at great peril to the success of the team.

I was dying to see all the other competitors, all the other countries at my first Worlds in Moscow. I was dying to see Joan Lind in Moscow. I was dying to see Moscow.

But I just couldn't do it.

I was dying just thinking about it.
My stomach was churning twenty-four hours a day at the injustice I was witnessing, and even my friend Larry Wittig wasn't talking to me, blaming me, I suppose, for my part in the farce.

And so, reluctantly, I resigned and headed back to my new home in Long Beach, more determined than ever to find a cure for PMD . . .

. . . for Pete Mallory's Disease.

* * * * *

Incidentally, I can report to you that today I remain invisible to Fairthy Farthington, as invisible as I am to John Hartigan, and have been so for twenty-seven years now.

Nowadays I read in *U.S.Rowing* that Fairthy Farthington is winning world masters championships just about every year.

Bravo Fairthy! Wasn't it predicted you would rise again and beckon?

Ponte Vecchio

So I returned early to Long Beach that summer and began coaching again in earnest, but I never stopped actually rowing, loved it too much.

Interesting thing about rowing and coaching at the same time. As I evolved, as I got a new idea, I had to take my own medicine. Whatever I told my crews, I had to test out and apply to myself as well. I don't know if I could have kept learning and growing in my understanding and appreciation of the sport of rowing without doing most of my coaching from the perspective of a single.

* * * * *

And I've had a good career as a coach, in retrospect better than I ever deserved. I've worked with men and women, from little kids through juniors and seniors and masters all the way to one incredibly old guy with one leg already in the grave.

Then one day he just wasn't there any more. His wife thanked me, told me rowing was the last joy he experienced on Earth before going to Heaven.

We should all be so lucky . . .

I've worked with lightweights and heavyweights, college and club, fast and slow, with a lot of winners, and a select few very deserving losers, oh yes. I've worked with the good, the bad, the ugly. I've touched a lot of lives, made a lot of friends . . . who I value as life itself.

> *"There's nothing worth the wear of winning*
> *But laughter and the love of friends."*
> - Hilaire Belloc

Rowing is family for me, and that's a favorite quote of my Dad's, who once organized and rowed in the bow seat of a boat he named "the Gentlemen's Eight." Top hats and canes on their shirts. What a crack-up! Seen a picture. Wish I could have been there in person.

Now I don't want you to get the wrong impression about my father. He was indeed a very gregarious guy. He had a *lot* of friends, bushel baskets full, in fact, but he also had his share of adversaries, and he dealt with them eloquently.

He is the man who taught me to say *"trente-six fois merde."*

My father's most treasured quote:

"That prick of misery!"
- Homer

It's from the *Iliad*. Look it up, but you'll need an old translation. The newer ones sanitize the language. Dad translated the *Iliad* from the original Greek at Kent, so he knew all the juicy stuff.

My Dad is just a memory now, rowed his last race, as it were, but he left behind a full measure of both friends and p's of m.

I, too, have acquired my own set of both in full measure. (With more of both to come with this book, I'll hazard a guess!)

Truth be told, I really don't have what it takes to be a good coach. I'm an anachronism. I'm way too inflexible, too impatient, too intolerant. My odyssey has been way too personal, and the intensity of my search for perfection in rowing (and in life) has driven me to step on more than a toe or two along the way.

I've made *way* more than my fair share of mistakes!

To most of you I have offended, I offer my regrets and sincere apologies.

> *"Chuck, I only said you were ACTING like an asshole.*
> *And whether you were or you weren't, who can remember?*
> *Who cares? That was twenty years ago, for Heaven's sake!*
> *Please, please forgive me."*
>
> - a contrite Peter Mallory

To a few of you . . . well, to a few of you . . . I wish I could be more charitable.

But I can't. So go ahead and hate me.

You have a perfect right.

I deserve it. So do you.

Despite my personality flaws, during my journey I've coached fifty national champion crews.

114

And the first American junior women's crew ever to win an international championship.

Altogether, five Worlds appearances.

Of the nine cox'n positions on the U.S. Women's Olympic Teams of 1976, 1980 and 1984, women who had begun their careers with me filled five of those slots.

Darn proud of that particular statistic, I can tell you!

I've coached in four languages. I've visited Pocock Racing Shells in Seattle, *Stämpfli* in Zurich, *Schönbrod* in Biddeford, *Empacher* in Eberbach. I've known Jacob Kaschper and Howard Croker, Wayne Neal and Rigger Brown.

Joe Burk and Ted Nash and Ana Tamas and Tom McKibbon have coached *me*.

My good friend Jack Frailey once told me I actually said something thoughtful he didn't already know, but, then again, maybe he was just being charitable.

Jim Barker helped me make weight once, and I sounded like Mickey Mouse for a day and a half.

I kid you not!

I've lived long enough to see Montgomery/Ward in a double and Coffey/Staines in a pair.

Here's something only people from the West Coast will get, a regional in-joke, if you will:

Once, years ago at a regatta site, when someone came over and asked to borrow a particular tool, I got to say:

"Go see Cal."

I've been within zero degrees of separation from Tote Walker, Melch Burgin, Karl Adam, Allen Rosenberg, Frank Cunningham, Bill Stowe, Boyce Budd, Harry Parker, Tiff Wood, Tony Brooks, Monk Terry, Pete Raymond, Jack Kelly, Aldina Nash, Tommi Keller, Nelly Gambon, Shealy and Cashin, Hough and Johnson, McKibbon and Van Blom, Cromwell and Storm, Nunn and Maher, Finley and Ferry, Lea and Knecht.

Heroes all.

(Hardly a woman on that list. My apologies. Weren't too many in the sport during my era of oarsmen and not oarspersons.

They've come a long way since then. Me, too. Probably coached more good women than good men in my lifetime.)

I can put a grip on a sculling oar all by myself out standing in my field. Can you?

I've rowed with Dave Vogel and Scott Roop and Bob Rogen. I've coached Mick Feld and Brad Alan Lewis and Lynn Silliman.

When she was fifteen years old and had just flipped the single I lent to her, I told a sopping wet Sarah Garner she'd be a world champion one day.

True story.

All by themselves, my junior pair of Margi Fetter and Betsy Zumwalt opened a can of ass-whup on our own United States Rowing Association after their board of directors unilaterally declared a boycott the 1979 Moscow Junior World Championships.

Dammit, that was sweet!

After losing every single step in the U.S. Olympic Committee-mandated grievance procedure, after dragging the process out for more than six months, the United States Rowing Association finally took my girls to binding federal arbitration.

The attorney arguing in favor of the boycott was the federation's big star, world silver and Olympic bronze medalist Anita de Frantz, a role model for both my girls and me, and a fellow Shortridge Blue Devil and fellow Hoosier (Is this a small world or what?), but younger than I, so I suppose both Kurt Vonnegut and I missed running into her in Indianapolis, Indiana.

My sister Betsy didn't. She, too, is a fellow Shortridge Blue Devil and fellow Hoosier, and she walked the hallowed hallways the very same years that Anita did.

My fellow Hoosier parents didn't. They went to the very same church that Anita and her parents attended.

Strange to find myself and my team opposed by a family friend, especially by Anita de Frantz, us being fellow Shortridge Blue Devils and fellow Hoosiers and all, and *extra* especially on the subject of something as patently ridiculous and destructive as an athletic boycott.

The federal judge in arbitration summarily brushed aside the feeble arguments of our own United States Rowing Association, as presented by a very uncomfortable Anita de Frantz.

Sorry, Anita. That's what you get for becoming a lawyer!

U.S. Junior Champions and U.S. Trials winners and U.S. Arbitration winners
Margi Fetter and Betsy Zumwalt in Moscow!

So, after the United States Rowing Association actually went to a *second* federal judge and tried to get the binding arbitration set aside, and after the new federal judge threatened to put the entire board of directors in jail for contempt of court if they didn't stop their nonsense (I wonder just what part of *binding* they didn't understand?), after all that . . . we finally got to go to Moscow and compete.

Dammit, that was sweet!

But did anybody learn anything? I'm afraid not.

If only that were the end of the story.

In one of those *delicious* ironies provided to us by life, just one year later the proverbial shoe ended up on the proverbial other foot.

Anita de Frantz herself became one of the most visible and vocal victims of the United States Government's boycott of the Moscow Olympics.
For a couple of weeks you couldn't turn on the TV without seeing her sad face.
And, unlike Margi Fetter and Betsy Zumwalt in 1979, there was to be no rescue in federal arbitration for old Anita de Frantz in 1980.
Nosirree!
Who says there is no God? No Old Testament "eye for an eye" God?

I laughed out loud!

. . . that is when I wasn't crying for Anita and all the other innocent athletes on our 1980 Olympic Team, gymnasts and swimmers and runners and jumpers and wrestlers and field hockey players, more than a few of them personal friends of mine!
Innocent athletes who were so cruelly punished by our foolish government.

True story.
I kid you not!

Needless to say, in November, 1980, I did *not* vote to re-elect Jimmy Carter as President of the United States.

Anyway, Anita had to settle for becoming Vice President of the International Olympic Committee, settle for becoming the most powerful woman in sport on Earth today!
Absolutely true story.
Couldn't make this stuff up.

(I've been within zero degrees of separation from Anita de Frantz. She counts. *She is an authentic hero!*)

I know that saying "crew team" is like saying volleyball ball or Rio Grande River or Department of Redundancy Department. A crew already *is* a team, for Heaven's sake!

I know a scull is always an oar and never a boat, so you can *never* go out and "row a single scull."
Sorry, "John Biglen in a Single Scull." Sorry, Thomas Eakins.
A sculler takes two sculls from the scull rack, puts them in the port and starboard scull-locks, and rows a *shell* in the single sculls or double sculls or quadruple sculls *event.*
Every time! *No exceptions!*
Now don't go and look up "scull" in the dictionary! People have been getting this wrong so darn long now, for *centuries* now, for Heaven's sake, that many dictionaries are wrong now, too.

Come on! The word doesn't make sense any other way. Why are you being so close-minded? Make the world a better place today. Use the word correctly!

I've rowed the canals of Erie and Welland and Amsterdam and Bruges, I've rowed under the *Ponte Vecchio.* I've driven boat trailers over the Rockies, under the Alps, over the Dolomites. I've rowed on Seattle Slough and Lake Havasu, on Seneca and Cayuga and Quinsigamond, on the Schuylkill, the Raritan, the Housatonic, the Connecticut, at Harvard and Hazewinkel and Haderslev. I've been to Bled and Merced, Ghent and Kent, Dartmouth and Dortmund.
I even got to Moscow.
Prosit!

Never did get to Henley, though. Canadian Henley, oh my, yes! Royal Henley, alas, no.
Oh well.

I've had many rowers go on to great colleges, great careers. A couple of them have even won Olympic and world championships after I touched their lives.
They were my family. I poured my heart into them all . . .

. . . and I've told you . . . I figured it out . . . how to move boats . . . somewhere along the way I figured out what I had done so very wrong for Fred Leonard my senior year in college . . . and during my seat racing for Steve Gladstone . . . and now I can finally make boats move . . . me, Peter Mallory . . .

I finally learned how to move boats, Fred! . . .

I finally learned how to move boats, Steve! . . .

. . . and, best of all, I learned how to teach anybody how to do it right.

Too late for me in '67 and in '72 . . . too late for Pete Maxon in '73 . . . but not too late for a young girl named Denny Maloney from Bachelors Barge Club in Philadelphia.

When she really needed it, I was there!

A Paper Bag

It's 1978, and I am again at a National Team Selection Camp, but now I am in *charge* . . . and very much feeling this might be my great opportunity to atone for the myriad sins of 1973.

Sins of omission and commission.

I am the U.S. National Junior Women's Sculling Coach.

Immediately after the Women's Nationals in Seattle, I hold a selection camp for the quad and double I will take to Belgrade, to the very first Worlds to include junior women.

Selection will be done by seat racing in cox quads.

During this time in my life I have been coaching at Mission Bay Rowing Association in San Diego, which I co-founded, and I have spent the entire year on my own visiting programs on both coasts, encouraging young scullers and their coaches. Of the top ten junior sculling candidates in the country that year, three are from my MBRA program and five more have received training schedules and extensive personal coaching from me. At various points during the season, four have rowed as "guests" in composite boats with my girls, and two of these adoptees, along with all three of my San Diego girls, have won gold medals for me at the Nationals.

But in my planning for the camp, the specter of Jacob Marley haunts me every night at midnight for an entire year . . .

> *"F. Fairthington Farthington,*
> *the Ghost of Team Camps Past . . ."*
> - apologies to Charles Dickens

I come to the conclusion that no matter how the selection process goes, there will be way too much opportunity for others to suspect me (and me to suspect myself) of favoritism if I am in any way personally involved with the selection process.

Period.

So I include on my staff two international-class cox'ns from my senior team at home. They are my good friend Alan Klier, a gangly, nervous fellow with piercing eyes, originally from the Northwest, along with Kelly Rickon, the cox of my very first national championship crew from ZLAC Rowing Club in San Diego, her Olympic silver medal still six years in the future.

"What's a ZLAC?" you might ask.
"Good question," I might reply.
Stands for Zulette, Lena, Agnes and Caroline, four nineteenth-century society ladies in starched collars and bloomers.
Back then the most prestigious social club in town was the San Diego Rowing Club.
"Men only! No women allowed!"
So Zulette, Lena, Agnes and Caroline started a rowing club of their own.
"Women only! No men allowed!"

Makes perfect sense to me!

For more than a hundred years now, the daughters of all the best families from the toniest neighborhoods in San Diego have become members of ZLAC Rowing Club and learned to row.
There are mothers and grandmothers and great-grandmothers and more by now. But, despite their unending love and undying loyalty, no mothers seemed to be naming their own daughters Zulette any more, that is, if they ever did . . .
. . . nor Lena nor Agnes for that matter.
Come to think of it, in all my years of coaching at ZLAC, and I was their first professional coach, I never even saw a single Caroline.
Not a one!
Saw three Olympians, though . . . and Kelly would be the third.

Kelly Rickon. Known her half my life . . . which is almost all of hers. Started her coxing at the age of fourteen. Seemed bewildered when she steered her ZLAC junior eight to *her* first, *their* first, and *my* first national title in Princeton in 1975.

> *"How could this be happening to me,*
> *Little Kelly Rickon from San Diego?"*
> - Little Kelly Rickon from San Diego

I can report with the benefit of hindsight that Kelly has kept a measure of that bewilderment into the 21st Century, now a wife and mother, working for the San Diego Crew Classic. Always astonished at her good fortune during her life to be continually surrounded by such good-hearted people, both in boats and out.

Indeed a lucky soul, don't you think?

* * * * *

No bewilderment for Kelly when she sits in a boat, though. Nosirree. And none for Alan, either.

By 1978 the two of them have years of experience conducting entire workouts, including seat racing, from their cox'n's seats without supervision from any coach.

At my selection camp they will perform the seat racing independently, out of sight of anyone, while I on the opposite shore will be, ready in my single . . . to run a development camp for everyone else . . . far away on a separate body of water.

After the very first session I meet back at the dock with Kelly and Alan, and they inform me that one major upset has already come out of seat racing, and it's a potential nightmare. Shades of Pete Mallory, Pete Maxon!

Now at the Nationals, my girls have come in first in the junior quad for the third year in a row, and first and second in the junior double for the third year in a row and have captured five of the six spots in the junior singles final!

So there!

But the national singles title has gone to an outsider, the aforementioned Denny Maloney, big and strong, but virtually a novice. It takes Alan and Kelly very little time to determine that despite her obvious talent and potential, Denny can't move boats, can't seat race her way out of a paper bag. No way she is going to make the team.

No way in *Hell*.

What a shame!

And what a waste! Probably the most gifted athlete of the lot. Isn't *her* fault she has no intuitive sense as to how to move a boat that includes teammates.

Add in that her coach has a volatile personality, is on the National Junior Committee *and* has been forcibly added to my camp staff, and I am feeling the pressure big time.

For lots of reasons it's time for me to do *something*. Right? But what? I have no role at all in selection . . .

Twice a day for the next three days I leave my single on shore and supervise the development camp from a double with Denny as my partner, sometimes in bow, sometimes in stroke. We work on everything. I explain to her the secret that is just beginning to emerge in my consciousness, the truths I am belatedly gleaning from Bill Wark and Chuck Crawford, from Pete Maxon and Fairthy Farthington, from Doc Councilman and Arthur Lydiard, from Dietrich Rose and Jim Moroney.

I teach Denny Maloney how to move a boat, and after three days I send her back to Alan and Kelly, and on that very last day of selection Denny earns the bow seat in the quad on her own.

On her very own.

That summer we win the *petite finale* at the Worlds in Belgrade. Photo finish. On the last stroke. On the Blue Danube. Long way from Philadelphia or Seattle or San Diego.

Couldn't have done it without Denny.

Happy ending for her and her teammates.

* * * * *

Incidentally, Denny making the team meant one of my three original San Diego girls didn't. Simple arithmetic. Barbara Beaudette would be left home as we made our way to Germany and Austria and Yugoslavia.

Oh, the adventures she missed!

And by the thinnest of margins!

At the end of the selection camp after the team had been announced, I got an incredibly nasty phone call from Barbara's father, all about loyalty and breaking up a team and the bond between Barbara and her San Diego teammates, who were now leaving her behind.

124

And he didn't even know how much I had done, albeit indirectly and unintentionally, to help bring about the downfall of his daughter.

Tough on me.

Bob Beaudette's in Heaven now. I hope he's forgiven me.

Barbara became a model and married an Italian noble.

photo credit: Peter Mallory

1978 U.S. Junior Women's Quad, Worlds *Petite Finale* Winners
Bow Denny Maloney, Bachelors Barge Club; Ann Strayer, Phillips Academy/
Mission Bay; Margi Fetter, Mission Bay; stroke Betsy Zumwalt, Mission Bay; cox'n
Barbara Oldershaw, Berkeley High School/Oakland Strokes.

Guaranteed Employment

If you're a coach or a rower, I suppose just about now you want to know what I taught Denny Maloney during those three days in a double.

You want to know what the secret of boat moving is.

I probably should rephrase that. You're probably curious to find out what I **think** the secret is . . . because 99.44% of you won't believe me anyway, even after I tell you.
Isn't that grand?

> *"Who is so deafe or so blinde as is hee*
> *That wilfully will neither heare nor see?"*
> - John Heywoodes Woorkes, 1562

Steve Gladstone, a man who kisses his wife and child every evening when he gets home from the Cal boathouse, a thoughtful man, an intense man, but a man who puts his pants on one leg at a time, just like you and I, my lifelong friend Happyrocks calls it guaranteed continued employment for him . . . and he's very grateful.
As long as so many coaches in the world continue to ignore what has been right in front of their noses during their entire lifetimes, regular guys like Steve Gladstone will continue to enjoy an "unfair advantage," and everyone else will continue to wonder how the heck they do it.

So, in the interest of fair play (and book sales), I'm going to reveal to you Steve's "unfair advantage." I'm going to tell you the secret of moving boats.

But Steve reminds you that it's more than just moving boats. It's about having an open mind and a real interest in learning, something that doesn't come easily in rowing . . . or any other human endeavor, as far as he or I can tell.

Even Steve Gladstone has an "if only" story:
"In all the years I spent at Cal, beginning in the fall of 1972, I only spoke to Ky Ebright a couple of times.

"Ky Ebright had coached the Golden Bears for thirty-seven years, had coached them to three Olympic eights gold medals, and it never even occurred to me to engage this man in a single meaningful conversation.

"I wasn't even curious. After all, I was already successful. What more did I need to know?

"Now, in retrospect, I need to ask . . .

"What the Hell was I thinking?"

* * * * *

So curiosity came late to Steve Gladstone.
Too late to talk with Ky Ebright. He's in Heaven now.

How 'bout you? How curious are *you*? More importantly, how *open-minded* are you?

No Power, Pete

I *will* tell you the secret . . . but in my own good time. First you have to appreciate just what you're up against.

I tell you this: the prejudice against effective boat moving in America runs long and deep.

I'll repeat that. **The prejudice against effective boat moving in America runs long and deep!**

In John VIII, 32, Jesus of Nazareth said, "The truth shall make you free."

Here's another quote:

> *"The truth which makes men free is for the most*
> *part the truth which men prefer not to hear."*
> - Herbert Sebastian Agar

Not surprisingly, I'm reminded of a story. It takes place during my year of coaching at Cal State Long Beach.

* * * * *

You may recall I spend my very first morning in California participating in the Long Beach Rowing Association sculling workout. Among my new teammates are Joan Lind, my Athena, grey-eyed goddess, who had captured my heart as we raced throughout Europe the year before, and John Van Blom, 1969 European doubles champion.

John's '69 doubles partner, Tom McKibbon, a Renaissance man, a metaphysical man, is coaching.

McKibbon and Van Blom. Gods who walk amongst us humans . . .
Gods who smile and welcome me into their world.

Pinch me.

I am greeted by Dawn and her rosy-red fingers.

The morning workout is a series of six 500-meter sprints . . . and with me not having rowed in real competition for many months! On pure adrenaline I am fast, very fast in fact, for the first two 500s . . . and then reality sets in.

Still, I'm in Heaven, and everyone's *so* nice!

Afterward, the whole group goes to breakfast together, and that's when I first meet a fellow named Greg Lahkso, warm and bubbling with enthusiasm. During the workout he and McKibbon had been tracking the boats on bicycles, Greg helping with stopwatches and things.

Obviously he is great friends with everyone.

As the weeks go by we become almost inseparable, both of us adding comic relief to the efforts of Joan and John as they prepare for the coming World Championships.

Yes, John Van Blom will also qualify for Moscow, he as the U.S. men's single sculler.

I am surrounded by the best our country has to offer.

One afternoon Greg and I are at the boathouse together, he helping me repaint a rack full of blades the traditional Cal State Long Beach Yellow and Brown in preparation for my debut as Varsity Lightweight Coach in the fall. Turns out Greg had just recently graduated from CSULB, where he had rowed on the heavyweight JVs.

Gee, he's my size: 5' 11" and maybe 165 pounds? Why didn't he row on the lightweight squad? He might have been a star!

He tells me the lightweights at State have no prestige. He preferred being on the heavy JVs.

I'm not surprised or offended. It's a common affliction. I've heard the same story lots of times at lots of boathouses. It is the fate of all lightweights to be ever unrespected, ever unappreciated. I assure Greg that *my* team will be a team he would kill to be a part of, a champion team, an undefeated team, a team to be respected like no other Cal State Long Beach team in history, past, present or future, heavy or light.

Brave words from a brash, young coach. No wonder I am destined to make no great friends among State heavyweights this year.

Fast forward to the following spring.

Greg and I aren't seeing that much of each other any more. Both been busy. Sometimes he comes out in my coach's launch for a practice.

The college season is fast coming to a close, and just as I promised our varsity eight is undefeated, never headed, never winning by less than a length.

And my eight is made up of the fastest freshman four on the West Coast, heavy or light, by ten seconds, and the fastest varsity four on the West Coast, heavy or light, by eighteen seconds! Faster than Orange Coast, Cal, U-Dub, you name it, faster than everybody.

Think about that a moment as I pause to pat myself on the back!

I am bursting with plans for the future and already looking forward to our summer program, aiming to win the U.S. Trials in the lightweight coxless four event.

I have already recruited Rod Johnson, stroke of the 1973 undefeated UCLA Lightweights, John Phelps from my 1972 Penn Freshman Lightweights, and now I'm working on Greg to join the summer squad. In fact I have been working on him all winter, telling him it's his chance to be more than a friend and camp follower to great rowers but to actually achieve greatness himself, to row in what will be a magnificent four.

For some reason, he's a tough sell . . .

I finally convince Greg to join us for a special Sunday morning practice in his honor. I put him in a coxless four with my three best guys. He's a bit rough, a bit rusty, but together they are faster than the other four, and both boats leave in the dust my undefeated JV eight!

I'm so proud of my guys, and I'm so proud to be able to share this rowing experience with my first best friend in California.

After the workout I don't press him until we sit down together for breakfast.

"Well? . . . What do you think? Pretty awesome, huh?"

Greg pauses.

"I hated it," he says, embarrassed to be hurting my feelings.

I am stunned. I ask him why.

130

"Why, Greg? Why?"

He gathers steam. "There was no power, Pete, no *excitement!* I guess rowing with heavyweights my whole career has spoiled me, but when I go up to the catch, I've come to expect an absolute explosion of effort, the boat jumping and shuddering in response.

"I want to *feel* my teammates attacking their oars, experience their shafts straining and bending." His eyes sparkle. His passion is remarkable.

He continues. "I expect the boat to leap ahead. That four today just didn't do that. It just, I don't know, just cruised. I guess it's too much to expect anything more from mere lightweights . . ."

My heart sinks.

I think to myself, "Now I sure don't feel like an expert in boat moving yet. There's a lot I still don't understand . . . but, dammit, **that four that Greg just rowed in this morning was probably faster than the precious JV heavyweight eight he rowed in last year!** That's got to count for something!"

Not with Greg.

* * * * *

As I promised him, my Cal State Long Beach Lightweight Varsity Crew finishes the season the undefeated 31-0 Western Sprints champions, the most successful State crew ever.

Ever.

Before or since.

We begin raising money for our planned trip to Henley in England the following year. I am finally going to Henley!

And as I promised, we go forward with our summer program and put together a magnificent lightweight coxless four. We win the Canadian Henley . . . but then lose the U.S. Trials, mostly due to my own inexperience peaking crews at this lofty level of competition.

After the trials, I feel like I have let the guys down. In Canada, before I overtrained them and we experienced a couple of injuries, we were effortlessly faster than the trial winners have turned out to be, and those guys go ahead and win a world bronze!

Risen to the level of my incompetence, that's me, that's for sure.

1974 Long Beach Rowing Ass'n, Canadian Henley Champions, 155-Pound Four
Bow John Fletcher, Ted Beatty, Roy Boy Beard, stroke Rod Johnson.

But then again, within three years, two of my four guys, Rod Johnson and John Fletcher, make the National Lightweight Eight and win world medals on their own. So I guess we accomplished a thing or two after all. Bravo, guys!

* * * * *

And what became of Greg, the man who turned his back on my program because my world-class lightweights didn't hit the catch as hard as his mediocre college heavyweights?

The final irony:

At the end of the summer, my dear friend Ed Graham, the man who hired me on the spot to coach the lightweights at Cal State Long Beach the previous year, the man who even invited me to live in his house, unexpectedly retires as head coach of the college. I hurry home from the trials and apply to fill the vacancy, but my arrogance during the year has made me few friends on campus, and a State grad whose name I've now forgotten (Thank you, Dr. Freud!) is soon selected.

A former teammate of Greg's, as I recall. Had brown hair, slicked back like an eagle's feathers.

This fellow's first act as head coach is to fire me, telling me frankly and dispassionately that the Long Beach community isn't large enough to support two championship crews from the college and that his heavyweight team won't abide competition from my Henley-bound lightweights. His boys will rule the roost by making sure they have no competition.

At least he's honest.

(He's probably also heard what a jerk I am. No secrets in a boathouse, you know.)

Anyway, guess who the new head coach picks to supervise the dismantling of my championship lightweight program.

That's right. My good friend Greg Lahkso.

And Greg proves more than equal to the job, I can tell you. This man, who has no respect for lightweights, leads *my* lightweight program right back to the dreadful state from which I had raised it a year before.

Incidentally, I hasten to add, smugly, that next year, under that new head coach, the Cal State Long Beach Heavyweight Crew also totally *sucked!*

There *must* be a God!

* * * * *

But now I feel guilty. Of all the fine athletes I coached at Long Beach, all the kind people I met, here I go and write a book a quarter-century later, and almost the only guy I've mentioned by name so far is, of all people, Greg Lahkso.

> *"I won't have sons of bitches who are afraid*
> *to fight stinking up this place of honor!"*
> - General George Patton, United States Army

Believe me, I mention Greg only because his mindset is the norm in American rowing, even today.

Greg Lahkso *is* American rowing!

And why not? There are so many examples of great rowers tha apply power to their oars like Thor wielded his hammer.

For instance, Ted Nash.

But Ted, you are going to have to wait. I must assuage m conscience. I must offset an overdose of Greg Lahkso with a dose o Bob Rogen.

Ten Little Indians

Most of you will never meet Bob Rogen. Your loss. These days he's up in Sacramento, California, still rowing, still competing, still helping out with a bit of coaching. I wonder if anybody up there has a clue as to who they are sharing their dock with.

"What's so special about Bob . . . What's-His-Name?" they might inquire.
"I'm so glad you asked," I might reply.

* * * * *

Bob Rogen is the first returning athlete I meet when I take over at Cal State Long Beach in the fall of 1973. He heads straight down to the boathouse a day before school starts, can't wait like all the rest until the first scheduled practice.
He's *that* psyched.

Hadn't been a star the previous spring. Oh no!
Hadn't made the varsity boat.
Hadn't even made the JV.
No, Bob Rogen was the Rodney Dangerfield of the 1973 Long Beach State Lightweights. He spent the previous spring in the lightweight cox four, the equivalent of living with the pigs in the barn at the Walton's farm.
And he spent much of that spring in a rubber suit, for Bob was a husky boy. I saw a picture of that four somewhere along the line. They have obviously just lost some race, and Bob has a scowl on his face . . . like he hated life, which apparently at the moment of the photo he actually *did!*
No scowl on Bob's face when I meet him just a few months later. As I have told you, this guy is *psyched.* He sees nothing but promise for the coming year.
But, then again, so do I. For both of us a new beginning.

There had been no one slower than the Cal State Long Beach Lightweights the previous year, but I have almost the entire varsity and JV boats returning.

Good news, bad news.

Anyway, I go out and recruit a hundred new guys. In crew, you know what they say:

"The moe the merrier."
- John Heywood, again

I beg the experienced returnees to have patience with me as I teach the new guys to row.

I beg the experienced returnees to have patience with me as I ask them to do some things they've never done before, things like working hard and running and lifting weights and rowing with style.

Stuff like that.

I beg them . . . but to no avail. Just like the ten little Indians in the nursery rhyme, one by one they just melt away.

"And then there were none!"

Eventually the previous year's varsity is completely gone, and there is just a single solitary individual left from the JV, a fellow named Fred Mayfield . . . and, oh yeah, there's Bob Rogen from the Four.

Well, when seat racing is completed the following spring, what do you know, Bob Rogen has squeaked into the last available seat of the 1974 varsity eight.

From the worst lightweight four in the West one year to the best lightweight eight in the *history* of the West the very next.

Boggles the mind . . . but that's Bob Rogen.

And being the last man to make the boat means he's "on the bubble," just like at the Indianapolis 500, as I'm sure all you fellow Hoosiers can well appreciate.

Whenever Fred Mayfield or anybody else asks for a shot at the varsity, Bob is the one who has to fend off the challenge.

A week doesn't go by when Fred or someone else doesn't come up to me and announce that he is ready to kick Bob's ass.

Bob Rogen. The Rodney Dangerfield of the 1974 Cal State Long Beach Lightweights.

I can report to you with some satisfaction and a great deal of admiration that nobody *ever* kicks Bob's ass. Bob never loses, not even once . . . but that's Bob Rogen.

His reward? A San Diego Crew Classic gold medal, an undefeated season, a Western Sprints championship, so many shirts he almost disappears under the pile.
But that's Bob Rogen.

But that's not what makes Bob Rogen special. Oh no. After all, there are eight other people in that 31-0 boat, seven of whom can beat Bob in a seat race.

No, what makes Bob special was that when Greg Lahkso takes over the program the following year, *when absolutely everybody else quits,* Bob sticks around for his senior year. Says something about owing it to his college and to his sport.
"I guess I owe it to my college . . . and to my sport."

From the worst lightweight crew in the West to the best lightweight crew *in the history of the West* back to the worst lightweight crew in the West, all in three years' time.
Boggles the mind . . . but that's Bob Rogen.

And that's why Bob Rogen's so special.

A Hiccup

Time to talk about a man who personifies ideal rowing *ala* Greg Lahkso. Time to talk about Ted Nash.

Ted Nash is one of those larger-than-life personalities, someone who leaves his mark on you, on history. I first lay eyes on him in the weeks before the 1964 Olympics in Tokyo.

Vesper Boat Club has won the '64 Olympic Trials in the eight-oared event. Harvard was the year's best collegiate eight, but they lose in the trials to Vesper.

The Harvard stern four then comes back to win the cox four trials, while Ted Nash and his teammates from Lake Washington in Seattle earn the right to represent our country in the coxless four.

Before our three Olympic entries, the eight and the two fours, cox and coxless, get on the plane for Japan, the Olympic Committee decides to hold a scrimmage for them in Philadelphia. Lake Washington and Harvard will combine their fours into an eight to take on Vesper.

Well, you can imagine the excitement amongst the locals. On the appointed day my teammates and I hurry up East River Drive to the Schuylkill River finish line to witness this true battle of the titans.

Now we have to pause a moment to consider these two fours that are united into one eight: Ted and his guys are in their late twenties or even thirties, military types, short hair, physically mature, imposing, ruthless and direct in their approach to power application.

By contrast, the Ivy Leaguers are virtual children, undergraduate pretty-boy GQ preppies. Ted takes over and relegates the kids from Cambridge to the four seats in the bow of the composite eight.

Now, rowing is usually pretty much an anonymous sport, you know, the team before the individual and all that. But not when it comes to Ted Nash. We sit by the finish line, straining to see the two crews passing side-by-side under the Strawberry Mansion Bridge nearly a mile upstream. Vesper is obviously on the left . . .

. . . but what in the Wide World of Sports is going on in the composite boat?

The seven man. The arch of his back. The kooky hat that looks like it had been through a couple of jungle guerilla wars. The thrust of his head! It's a wonder the hat even stays on.

Painful to watch! Mind boggling! I think of a mad conductor looming over his orchestra. I think of a mutant Snow White towering over Seven Dwarfs.

"That *must* be Ted," someone gasps. We've already heard he will soon be coaching at Penn. "That's *got* to be him," someone else agrees, awe in his voice.

Now awe doesn't come easily to us. After all, we Penn men share the dock every day with the Vesper eight, each and every one a deity, bodies from *La Cappella Sistina*, all soon to become Olympic champions.

Boyce Budd looks like an enormous Yale Bulldog, which, coincidentally, is exactly what he is.

The Amlong brothers, both on active duty, wear their uniforms to the boathouse . . . and we feel like saluting and dropping for ten.

"Sir, yes *sir!*"

Even the kid of the group, Stan Cwiklinski, only looks like a kid until you sneak over and stand next to him and realize he has to stoop his head and step sideways through doors.

We half expect each of these guys to have an ax and a blue ox at home.

And indeed, Vesper narrowly wins the race this day. But this day we have a new superhero.

We only see Ted Nash.

Now think about this. You've got to be pretty darn heavy-handed to be clearly visible in a crowd of giants from 1,000 meters away. Look up "hammer" in a rowing dictionary, and you'll find a picture of Ted Nash.

* * * * *

I didn't know it back then, at the moment I first laid eyes on him as a blip on the horizon, but Ted and I were destined to have a long and stormy relationship, probably from the start, and he took dead aim at me more than once in the years that followed.

But I have never found it within me to dislike him. He probably won my heart forever the night he invited me to dinner at his house about a week after he returned to Philadelphia from Tokyo to assume his position as the new coach of the Penn Freshmen Heavies.

* * * * *

It's early October of my sophomore year. The semester is already well under way. The Olympics took place in September, and so one week I'm watching Ted Nash on television, the next he's asking for my help recruiting a team of freshman heavyweights from out of the Penn dorms.

My help.

And he's absolutely right to come to me and my teammates. We lightweights know every hallway, every nook of every dorm. We get him his team in no time flat, and the dinner invitation follows.

After a delightful meal, his beautiful wife, Aldina, clears the table, and Ted begins to reminisce, holding us spellbound.

He wins an Olympic gold medal on Lago Albano in Rome four years earlier in the coxless four event, organizing and training the three strapping military types who are his teammates. When they all come home, everyone but Ted promptly retires.

Undeterred, Ted recruits three new guys, teaches them, trains them, coaches them, toes the boat himself from the three seat, and qualifies to represent the U.S. a second time in Tokyo.

Isn't that a great story?

It gets better.

As he describes it, his new Lake Washington four is mid-way through its Olympic qualification heat in Tokyo when they realize something is terribly wrong. One of their mates is faltering. Soon the man has stopped altogether. He has to be rushed to the hospital for an emergency appendectomy.

What to do? That evening Ted takes stock of the situation. The U.S. team has brought a spare to Japan for just such an emergency, but he's a Harvard boy, not even good enough to have made the Harvard cox four.

But what other choice is there? Their last chance to qualify for the final is fast approaching. What choice do they have?

Ted and his teammates graciously welcome the new boy into the boat. His whole approach to rowing is the antithesis to Lake Washington's, but Ted reports to us that he is a quick learner. The boat barely qualifies but keeps on improving.

The day of the Olympic final . . .

Ted pauses, reflecting. He has us on the edge of our seats.

"Well, how did it turn out?" We can contain ourselves not a moment longer.

"We got the bronze, less than a second behind the winners . . ."

One second . . . Maybe fifteen feet? Behind the gold medalists?

". . . and only three feet behind the silver medalists."

. . . three feet? A meter after 2,000 meters?
. . . three feet. A heartbeat. A hiccup.

Three feet!

A . . . minute . . . of . . . silence . . . goes by in that room.

I have to ask:

"Did it make a difference, I mean, having the Harvard guy in there?"
Ted looks at the ceiling, rubs his chin as if it had never before occurred to him to ask himself this question.

There's deathly silence.

"Well . . . I suppose . . . we might have had a chance . . . at second place."

I loved Ted Nash for that answer. Still do.

Coincidences Like That

And that fellow who filled in? The Harvard spare?

Twelve years later I am sharing a cab from the Montreal airport to the 1976 Olympics with a very attractive couple I've never seen before. My Heavens, they're good looking, like models from *Vanity Fair* magazine!

I can't help listening as they chat pleasantly to one another. I soon figure he has to be a former rower, and we start talking.

Ted Nash's name comes up.   Turns out this was the guy, the 1964 spare!

Is this a small world or what?

For Heaven's sake, my life is like a novel by Henry Fielding!

I tell this guy Ted's version of their remarkable odyssey.
He's touched.

It's coincidences like that which convince me that there definitely is a God, He's definitely read *Tom Jones* and *Great Expectations*, He's *most* definitely a rower . . . and He must have a Hell of a sense of humor!

Excuse the pun.

Tora! Tora! Tora!

But back to Ted Nash.

Hard to criticize his technique. Hard to be anything but in awe of this larger-than-life icon.

After all, think of his success! Never seemed to occur to me or anybody else that maybe he was successful not *because of* but *despite* his approach to power application.

And so I rowed with as much Ted Nash-style fury as my lightweight body could muster.

I wonder if he ever noticed . . .

And why would I row like that?

Well, for one thing, everybody did. For another, I wanted to be as successful as Ted Nash! For a third, that's how Fred Leonard taught me.

Fred arrived at Penn and into my life at a moment of enormous change in American rowing. It was the same fall that Ted arrived at Penn, the same fall that Vesper became Olympic champions, the same fall when everyone was talking about a fabulous crew from West Germany.

Vesper beat Ratzeburg Rowing Club to win Olympic gold in Tokyo, but Ratzeburg was winning the war. Their coach, Karl Adam, was changing our sport, almost overnight. He had introduced a new hull design for racing shells, adjustable riggers, new rigging geometries, new blade shapes and oar lengths, weight lifting, cross training, training off season, etc., etc. The list goes on. Nothing was off limits for Karl Adam.

He introduced all this to a sport that hadn't come up with an original idea in 100 years. You know what his advantage was?

Get this.

He didn't know doodley squat about rowing!

That's right. He was a boxing coach. How about that?

I only heard him speak once, and it took me more than a decade to absorb what he actually represented. Karl Adam has become my hero.

143

Question the conventional wisdom!
Question everything!
        - Karl Adam (my paraphrase)

The sad thing is that most American coaches never got it with Karl Adam.

Walking out of a Karl Adam lecture in 1967, Stan Pocock, more thoughtful than most people in our sport, looked at the expressions of adoration on the faces around him and declared, "That just set back American Rowing ten years."

How prophetic.

Instead of following Karl Adam's spirit and example, instead of questioning orthodoxy like Karl Adam did, American coaches simply anointed him as the new orthodoxy. The "West German" style in place of the "American" style, *Karlisches*, *Donoraticos* and *Stämpfli*s instead of American Pococks, but that's not what concerned Stan Pocock.

No. Stan was concerned that nobody was learning anything It didn't occur to anybody to actually be thoughtful or reflective about rowing!

How Karl Adam must have laughed at us!

And now, with the advantage of decades of retrospect, I have come to realize that most American coaches back then also completely misunderstood Karl Adam's preferred rowing style.

My own coach, Fred Leonard, was certainly no exception.

Now it's true the Ratzeburg Style includes elongated tracks in the boat and a reliance on the use of more leg compression at the expense of less back swing. That much is obvious to the naked eye.

Add in all the weight lifting with the legs that Karl Adam recommended, all the power cleans, all the squats, and many of his disciples in America seemed to conclude that the Ratzeburg Style represented an opportunity to rely **even more** on American-style explosive leg drive to propel the boat forward.

And so they did. Harvard first, or so it seemed. Everybody following.

I'll tell you a secret. It wasn't true. Karl Adam neither believed in nor coached explosive legs.

Didn't do it!

Karl Adam neither believed in nor coached explosive legs!

Now think about that!

But I didn't realize this stunning revelation until I read an analysis of the various international styles of rowing, including the Ratzeburg Style, written by Prof. Dr. Theodor Koerner of East Germany nearly a quarter of a century later!

All I knew at the time was what Fred Leonard was teaching me. "Attack the catch with the legs!" More than ever, if that was possible.

"Attack! Attack! Attack!"

"Tora! Tora! Tora!"

Oh my, yes!

Throughout my college career I heard all my cox'ns call for "Power Tens" to increase explosive leg drive, and you can bet I moved Heaven and Earth to give it to them.

"Burn those legs!"

"Let me *feel* your catches, let me *feel* your leg drive!"

etc., etc.

Greg Lahkso would have felt right at home.

You, too, I'll venture to guess . . . because it's still happening today!

How Could They Be So Stupid?

With all this emphasis on explosive catches, explosive legs, naturally I assumed that for rowing my legs were my most important asset, and my arms were virtually useless.

So did everybody else, as far as I could tell.

The conventional wisdom.

The first time I set foot in the Harvard Boathouse was during the first Head of the Charles in 1965, and I was astonished to find there was actually an apparatus upstairs to increase arm strength.

"What a waste!" I thought. "How could they be so stupid?"

At the time, I wished I had stick figure arms so I could have even bigger legs and still make lightweight!

Picture me. A certain cartoon character *with* quads and *without* the forearms.

> "I fights to the finach
> 'Cause I eats me spinach!
> I'm Popeye, the sailor man!"
> - Popeye, the Sailor Man

And look at the way Harvard rowed, chins lifting, teeth clenched, heads thrown back at the catch. Allen Rosenberg, coach of that Olympic champion Vesper boat, described Harvard attacking each catch "as if they were trying to throttle a robber."

And I wanted to be just like them. Everybody did.

This was the guy Bill Wark had to contend with in a double?
Oh, my shame today!

Funny thing. The only Harvard boat I ever got to really get a good look at was the 1965 heavyweight varsity, so good that they and their coach, Harry Parker, made the cover of *Sports Illustrated*, trumpeted for all to see as "the World's Best Crew."

I saw them only once, from the top of the high bridge over the Severn River at half a mile to go on the Naval Academy rowing course.

146

They were lengths ahead of both Penn and Navy, and they looked so serene. I don't remember them attacking the catch.

Not a bit.

That's odd. Maybe they were just cruising. But look, they are at 36 with the bow man's puddle gliding past the cox'n, waaaaay past the cox'n, on each stroke.

That's some cruise!

And they make it look so eeeeasy. What swing! Isn't it odd the really great crews, apparently even the really great crews from Harvard, hardly look like they are working at all? So smooooth.

Greg Lahkso wouldn't be interested in rowing in a boat *that* boring!

Maybe I didn't understand Harvard as well as I thought I did.

Maybe nobody did.

Hmm!

(But I would have to wait seven more years for my conversation with Jim Moroney.)

The week after Harvard got on the cover of *Sports Illustrated*, they went off to Henley . . .

. . . and Vesper beat them . . .

. . . and then Ratzeburg beat Vesper!

Sports Illustrated curse.

And confusing!

Fool That I Was

And around that same time, some scientist puts load sensors on the oarlocks of a Penn varsity shell. Pull hard, and one light comes on. Pull harder, and you get two lights, etc., etc., up to four lights.

Well, the rowers quickly figure out the best way to light four lights is to pound the catch, explode with the legs, apply a power "spike."

And so they do.

And just as quickly Penn coach Joe Burk, who was Harry Parker's coach at Penn (Yes, Harry's a fellow Quaker. Is this a small world or what?) . . . anyway, Joe has been described as preferring strength over technique, but Joe quickly realizes the "Secret of the Lights." (Sounds like a *Hardy Boys* mystery.)

Joe realizes that the secret to making the boat go fast is not in how many lights you light . . . but in how *long* you keep them lit on each stroke . . .

. . . and that's *impossible* to do if you pound the catch.

Hmm!

* * * * *

But none of this interested me in the slightest, fool that I was back then. All I focused on was doing what I was told by Fred.

It's funny. Looking back on my life in rowing, all the clues were there from the very beginning. Still, it took me two decades . . . but I finally put it all together.

I don't think I could have done it had I not seen it graphed on a computer, because so much of what I have learned is the exact opposite of what I was taught, the exact opposite of conventional rowing wisdom.

The exact opposite.
Imagine that!

148

Killing Fish

Anyway, here it is. Hold on to your hats!
Here's the secret of boat moving.

I was taught to explode at the catch. So were you.

So were *you!*

After all, it's the conventional wisdom. Old as life itself:

> *"Who that well his warke beginneth,*
> *The rather a good ende he winneth."*
> - Gower: *Confessio Amantis*

Completely wrong!

Wrong in rowing, anyway. Doesn't work in a single . . . or a pair.
So why would it work in any other shell? The immutable laws of
physics are the same for all boats.
Aren't they?

And has everyone forgotten it is water we are attempting to move
through?
Watch water flow in a babbling brook, flowing over rocks and
around obstructions. Look at canyon walls eroded by a stream.
Water intuitively follows the path of least resistance. Water abhors
sharp edges, wears them down, smoothes them out.
Stand on the rim of the Grand Canyon. Check it out.
Oh yes. Water wins in the end. You can't fight water.
Period.
A rower must become one with the water environment. "You must
not do battle with the water, Grasshopper. You must become its ally, its
little brother. Or sister. You must respect it as your father . . . or mother,
and you must earn its trust and respect in return."

Said one rower to another years ago: "You're just out there
hammering the water. You're killing fish, not rowing."

I rest my case.

You must smooth out your rough edges. You must accelerate your oar smoothly and evenly from entry until release of each stroke. You must listen to the boat when it speaks to you . . . and it will!
Oh yes. You must practice the Zen of Rowing.
You must *grok* the water.

Mallory's First Law of Hydrodynamics: You must surge smoothly through the water!

Surge.
I know. Tough sell for all you macho rowers, you ergomaniacs.
Surrrrge.
Let the onomatopoeia roll over your brain.
Imagine the Cat Woman saying, "Suuuurrrrge!"

Now I'm by no means the first person to come to this conclusion, despite its heretical sound to most of you.
Those of you with sufficient curiosity can read directly Dr. Koerner of East Germany describing ideal international rowing style in the 1987 FISA Coaches' Conference publication. For those of you who are less enterprising, I'll paraphrase:

> *The athlete maintains steady pressure throughout the stroke, resulting in steadily increasing blade speed from catch to release. The intent is to accelerate the boat as long as possible, to impart as much speed as possible to the boat by the end of the stroke.*
> - Theodor Koerner, German Democratic Republic

And so Dietrich Rose and Jim Moroney had gotten it *right!*

And Joe Burk, with his keeping four lights lit as long as possible, had gotten it *right!*

> *"Si finis bonus est, totum bonum erit."*
> - Gestæ Romanorum

Two-thousand-year-old advice.   And the Romans were good rowers, too! Just ask General Lew Wallace.

And so no explosive legs.
Read my lips.
No explosive legs.

"No way!" you might say.

> *"Way!"*
> - Wayne Campbell

I've nicknamed my First Law of Hydrodynamics the "Leg Law," for your journey toward surging pullthroughs must begin right here with your legs.

Golden Opportunities

When I say, "Surge," I'm sure a few of you are saying, "Duh!"

To you, I am stating the obvious. Dr. Koerner was stating the obvious. Jim Moroney was stating the obvious.

"This is a big disappointment, Peter. There is nothing new here."

To you I say:

"AMEN!"

To you I say:

"WHERE THE HELL WERE YOU WHEN I NEEDED YOU IN 1967? IN 1972?"

The rest of you probably think I'm a lunatic for even suggesting there is a better way than your precious explosive leg catches, but I challenge you, *I challenge you*, to set aside all your rowing preconceptions for just one minute.

Perhaps for the first time in your life.

Use the Reasonableness Principle!

"What's the Reasonableness Principle?" you might ask.

Just this: Re-examine absolutely everything with a new eye, a fresh perspective! If it sounds reasonable, then dammit, don't reject it out of hand, no matter how unorthodox it may appear. If it doesn't sound reasonable once you give it a good critical look, question it immediately, even if nobody else does, even if nobody else *ever* has!

Even if it is universally accepted conventional wisdom!

Even if it is part of the *bedrock* of your own rowing philosophy!

Be Karl Adam.

Now I tell you this:

> *"Rowing has an infinite number of golden*
> *opportunities to apply the Reasonableness Principle!*
> *In this book we will only scratch the surface!"*
>
> - Peter Mallory

152

But let us continue with our current "for instance":

Even to you skeptics, doesn't surging power sound like a reasonable way to get through the water efficiently and economically?

Think about it. Doesn't it have some elegance, some intuitive *heft* to it?

"Then how did Ted Nash become Olympic champion?" you might ask. "He, sure as Hell, didn't surge!"

Let me give you a clue. They don't give style points in rowing. The winner is the boat that crosses the line first. How they got there, through finesse, through bludgeoning their victims into submission, or whatever else they did, doesn't matter a whit.

And even *I* understand that rowing is still eighty-five percent *or more* strength and fitness.

Look at Ted! He's the equal of any two or three of the rest of us mere mortals. If he washed up on shore, environmentalists would try to push him back out to sea!

Ted Nash won his Olympic gold medal the old fashioned way:

> *"Veni, vidi, vici."*
> - Julius Caesar

He came, he saw, he kicked everybody's asses, simple as that!

In my competitive days I never wondered how fast Ted might have been if he had been subtle and sensitive as well as strong and determined and direct.

Imagine Ted Nash rowing like Duvall Hecht.

Imagine!

Kind of takes my breath away today . . .

Incidentally, Ted may not have rowed with a lot of refinement, but he used his back like nobody's business. Ted Nash *did* surge. Ted Nash was *very* effective with an oar.

Quack! Quack!

In retrospect, I have to ask myself why did it take me so long to figure out that style counts? I have always appreciated elegant rowing.

Since I was a little boy.

Even before I ever laid eyes on a shell!

Since I was five years old.

* * * * *

It's dark outside, and there is frost on the bathroom window. The room is illuminated by a single bare light bulb in a receptacle above the mirror. The bathtub is an old free-standing cast iron and porcelain affair with tiger paws as feet, and in the tub I lie, up to my nostrils in water, a hippopotamus, dead still. . .

My rubber ducky floats nearby. Time passes. Life is good.

Eventually the water cools off.

Must I stir?

I am reluctant to disturb the glassy mirror surface that I survey from my vantage point just an inch above.

I gently reach forward, turn the hot water spigot and lie back down. The sound of cascading water is surprisingly loud. The ripples expand in concentric circles from the far end of the tub.

Soon, as it always does, the water around my feet becomes uncomfortably hot while the end up by my head remains uncomfortably cool. Nothing to do but mix the water.

And so my nightly childhood ritual begins.

I sit upright in the center of the tub, cup my hands and begin to coax the water into a circulation around me.

Left hand forward gently pulling back, right hand back gently pushing forward. Over and over.

Has to be just right to get the water flowing and not splashing over the sides.

The strokes go faster and faster.

Soon my rubber ducky has caught the current and races around me in a counter-clockwise direction. Around and around. It's mesmerizing . . . intoxicating.

"Up two, in two," a rubber ducky cox'n might say.

Now let's have some fun. Quick! Reverse the flow!

This takes skill and experience . . . which I have! The water seems confused for a moment, then bends to my will, this time racing clockwise. Faster and faster, until the water threatens the very top of the tub.

Rubber ducky, I love you.

I am a water sprite. I only stop when the hot water from the spigot has raised the temperature of the tub almost beyond bearing.

Reluctantly I turn the handle and settle back down, lobster red, as the water gradually regains its glassy smoothness. Ducky drifts aimlessly . . . then stops, looking the other way, ignoring me, disappointed our fun is over until tomorrow.

Quiet again. Life is very good.

* * * * *

Now I ask you. "What would my rubber ducky think of explosive catches?"

Would he not say they are unreasonable? that they seem out of step with his water environment, the only world he knows?

Would he not say . . . "Quack! Quack!" . . . ?

I think you know he would!

Everything

Years ago, as an athlete in search of explosive power application, I was taught my legs were most important, back next, arms least.

That's bass ackwards.

In order to achieve Koerner's surging pullthrough (Mallory's First Law of Hydrodynamics) arms, back and legs must combine into a unified, organic effort that leads to the oar steadily accelerating from entry to release. Muscle groups must be blended like music.

Like music.

If the piano is too loud or the drums too soft, it doesn't sound right. It's not music. Everything must be blended in just the right proportion.

The Golden Mean.

Proportion is everything! (Study suggestion: Highlight that last line.)

Aggressive legs can only interfere with the effort to achieve balance and proportion. Explosive legs overpower the back and arms and interrupt the flow. It remains important to have strong legs, so keep doing your leg presses and your squats, but in the boat during a race, the typical rower need only be aware of consistent squeeze down of the legs, lasting from the first instant to the very end of the stroke. Anything more, and the stroke loses its organic integrity.

In fact, legs can hurt more than help!

Now pause to reflect on that, pardner!

Physics is Physics

Now let's move on to the use of the back.

Back swing unifies the entire surging pullthrough, and it must begin right at the catch . . . along with the legs.

Right at the catch.

"Why?" you might ask.

"Why?"

You were taught differently, weren't you? Legs first, then the back. Right?

"Legs first" is *out*. "Explosive legs" is *out*. "Organic whole" is *in*.

Don't do anything at the catch you can't continue all the way to the finish. Squeeze the legs, and concurrently swing the back.

"Like a sculler?" you ask.

"Like a sculler," I reply.

We'll come back to this, I promise you.

In addition, the back must continue all the way to the finish.

"All the way?" you ask. "Why?

"Why all the way to the finish?" you protest. "Most people don't row that way. The back stops at some point, and the arms are left to finish the stroke unassisted."

"You are correct, sir. Most people don't row that way."

But they should!

Let me give you an opportunity to go out and test this assertion, a lab session to go along with my lecture.

Lesson plan:

Every crew I know either does the pick drill or has seen another crew doing it. Hold the legs flat, and don't use your sliding seat. Hold your back rigid in the "layback" position. Now row with the arms only: pick, pick, pick.

Lots of crews warm up using the pick drill. Thirty years ago the East Germans were the first to employ it, and everybody immediately copied them, assuming it must be good for something, but not knowing or caring exactly what it was designed to teach.

Heck, anyone who ever saw the East Germans row just wanted to row as well as they did.

Me, too!

Well, after several bottles of vodka in Moscow in 1979, I discovered my facility in German improved with every drink. And so, with my new-found fluency, I struck up a conversation with the entire East German national staff, also drunk and abnormally loquacious, and they told me the pick drill was originally intended to teach shoulder position in sweep rowing.

Isn't that interesting?

But back to our lab session. Let's use the pick drill to test the effectiveness of arm effort:

Do the drill in a single, in an eight, in any boat you like (but not in a scull!), or even on the ergometer. It matters not. They're all the same.

The same.

Now try to pull hard.

You can't. No leverage. The best you can do is maybe cheat with the back, maybe shrug your shoulders, but what you will probably end up doing when you really ratchet up your effort is draw your body into the oar instead of draw your oar into the body.

This is a common rowing flaw called "bucking the oar."

Now why would it be any different at speed, at the end of a full stroke? Leverage is leverage. Physics is physics.

Reasonableness Principle.

Bottom line is you just can't accelerate the boat with arms only. No leverage.

If you choose to finish the stroke with arms only, your two choices are: either forget about accelerating the boat and let the oar float to you . . . or buck the oar.

Only two choices.

Now if you haven't already done so, go try it. Seriously. You won't believe me until you prove it to yourself.

158

Put this book down and go out and try it. Do the pick drill. In a boat. On the erg. It matters not. All the same.

We'll reconvene once you have completed your lab assignment.

(Come to think of it, there *is* a third choice. You can just pull your oar out early and not finish the stroke. A lot of people, very successful people, actually do that . . . not finish the stroke.

Boggles the mind.)

Old Wine

I want to quote British Olympian Richard Burnell in his 1989 book, *The Complete Sculler:* "Once . . . the body has completed its backward swing, the sculler really has only his arms left. And, at the end of the working stroke, this is the moment when the boat must be accelerating to its fastest speed."

Good point, don't you think? Especially after your lab assignment.

Unfortunately, Burnell continues, "So it is really necessary to have the power of the arms at this point."

But the arms have no leverage on their own. You know this. You proved it.

And, according to Burnell (and Koerner, and Moroney, etc., etc.), this is "when the boat must be accelerating to its fastest speed."

We seem to have a major problem here, and so I submit to you that Burnell is wrong to encourage the rower to finish with arms alone. When the back stops swinging, the boat stops accelerating for that particular stroke. Simple as that.

Insight!

Conversely:

Mallory's Second Law of Hydrodynamics: The boat is moving only when the back is moving. (The "Back Law.")

Now don't shake your head. Dammit, this is not new! Despite the heretical sound of my conclusion, I didn't just make this stuff up.

Hell, none of this is new! None of my pretentious-sounding Laws of Hydrodynamics break any new ground! They're really not *my* laws at all.

"Old wine, new casks."
\- old proverb

To reinforce my point, let me quote Gilbert C. Bourne in *A Textbook of Oarsmanship,* 1925: "A good oarsman will so couple up the actions of the body and legs that they aid and reinforce one another **at every point of the stroke** . . . We mean that three powerful groups of muscles situated in the back, in the buttocks, and in the thighs **must be brought into action simultaneously at the beginning of the stroke, and must remain in action throughout the stroke**, mutually aiding and reinforcing one another." (my emphasis)

"Throughout the stroke!"

I repeat.

"Throughout the stroke!"

> *"Up your body, Peter!"*
> - Ana Tamas

So Ana had it right!

Now I'm aware this continuous use of the back flies directly in the face of the orthodox American rowing practice of leg drive first, back swing second and arms last on the pullthrough. Let me quote from what may be the most widely read description of "Proper Rowing Technique" in the entire world. The *entire* world!

> *"Begin the drive by pressing down your legs.*
> *Keep your arms straight and hold your back firm to*
> *transfer your leg power to the handle. Gradually*
> *bend your arms and swing back with your upper*
> *body, prying against the legs until you reach a slight*
> *backward lean at the finish. Pull handle all the way*
> *into your abdomen."*
> - Concept II Indoor Rower, Owner's Manual, p. 12

This **sequential** use of the various muscle groups is referred to throughout the world as **"the Rosenberg Style,"** in honor of my valued friend and mentor Allen Rosenberg, coach of that 1964 Vesper Olympic Champion Eight, and of the 1974 World Champion U.S. Eight (with Mike Vespoli in the four seat, by the way).

Allen Rosenberg.

It boggles my mind that there are now whole generations of rowers who have never heard of Allen Rosenberg, never met Allen Rosenberg, and may never ever do so. It boggles my mind that he took Vesper to Tokyo to win the Olympics before the vast majority of rowers in this country today were even born.

My God! I've become an old curmudgeon, and my book is a *history* book!

To most of you, Allen Rosenberg might as well be George Washington!

Do you know how some people seem to have faces carved from granite?

I don't have such a face.

Nineteen sixty-four Vesper stroke man Bill Stowe doesn't either, but his seven man Bill Knecht, now in Heaven, Bill Knecht did. Former Wisconsin coach Randy Jablonic doesn't. Navy coach Rick Clothier doesn't either. Former Dartmouth coach Pete Gardner does. Harvard coach Harry Parker definitely does.

Heck, it's common knowledge on the Harvard campus that God used Harry Parker's profile to create New Hampshire's Old Stone Face.

Well, Allen Rosenberg is another man who has a stone visage, but you might not notice it at first, for Allen is a very small man, no doubt a cox'n in his youth, and in our world of rowing where bigger is better, one might underestimate Allen Rosenberg on size alone.

And Allen Rosenberg has a smile that melts the hardness of his face.

Ever notice how some people don't meet your gaze? Well, Allen greets you with his tiny hand delivering a confident, firm grip. He looks straight at you, his brown eyes twinkling, and smiles a smile that tells you immediately that this man is sincerely interested in *you*.

Wonderful skill.

Only when he is looking off into the distance, like when he is coaching, can you detect the firmness of his resolve. This tiny person is a giant of a man.

And by the way, Allen's the other man in my experience to coach in a three-piece suit. Never a hair out of place, shoes always shined. Look up fastidious in a rowing dictionary, and . . .

* * * * *

162

I'll never forget attending a seminar given by Allen in 1975. He had mentioned "back splash" during the morning session.

I submit that back splash is a metaphor for Allen Rosenberg.

"What is back splash?" my son Philip asked me when I was teaching him to row quite a number of years ago. I tried to explain the phenomenon as well as Allen Rosenberg had explained it to me.

"Every time you put your oar into the water you must do it while you are still steadily gliding up the last inch or two on your seat track . . . and so you must urge the blade into the water while it is still traveling toward the bow of the boat.

"Therefore, the *splash* the oar creates as it enters the water will be off the *back* of the blade and toward the bow.

"*Back. Splash.*"

Well, my seven-year-old son was seething with anger, absolutely incensed that I should ask him to do something that so obviously would slow the boat down. It took him two full weeks before his mind stopped protesting and allowed him to trust me enough to actually try to back splash.

And another year to do it reliably.

"Now what does this have to do with Allen Rosenberg?" you might ask.

During the lunch break at that seminar, surrounded by adoring coaches, myself included, all of us hanging on his every word, Allen sat with perfect posture in a high-backed upholstered chair, one leg politely crossed over the other at the knee, trousers perfectly creased, a saucer and cup full of hot coffee held delicately in his left hand and a teaspoon in his right.

He was back splashing.

And not spilling a drop.

He told us every time he had a bowl of soup or a cup of coffee he practiced his back splash.

And he smiled his smile.

Bravura performance!

Can you imagine Ted Nash back splashing in a cup of soup?

I don't think so.

Only Allen Rosenberg could pull it off.

Why? I believe it's because he is as counterintuitive as back splashing is.

An unschooled rower, such as my son once was, automatically presumes that back splashing would be the same as putting the brakes on the boat on every entry.

In reality, any braking effect is negligible.

What's *really* important is that back splash eliminates "boat check," the phenomenon of the boat hesitating and slowing down abruptly when the rowers' seats reach the end of their tracks and rowers apply pressure to their foot stretchers to retard the seat motion while the boat is still running out.

And, if that weren't enough, back splash adds up to five percent to the effective length of the stroke in the water.

Double Benefit. But it's *completely* counterintuitive.

Allen Rosenberg is a neat little man in a suit with a nice smile and good manners.

But Allen Rosenberg is also a world champion, a driven man with iron will and a rigid view of what it takes to row properly. Disagree with him, and you will indeed see that he is made of granite.

Completely counterintuitive.

For those of you who will never get to meet Allen Rosenberg, my condolences to you, for this man has had more influence on rowing in America than any other single person in the second half of the 20th Century . . . and he would light up your day with a single one of his smiles.

He would also teach you to use your muscles sequentially during the rowing stroke.

And so, after a life long odyssey, I find myself respectfully and regretfully disagreeing with my mentor, my George Washington.

Find My Own Way

Remoras are those fish that swim below the mouths of sharks, feeding off scraps that fall their way.

That's me, all right. There's hardly an original idea in this book. Everything I have come to understand, every "new" insight that I share with you today has really come from studying the thoughts of those much greater than I, people like Karl Adam, like Peter Klavora and Ernst Herberger and Theo Koerner, like Harry Parker, and, perhaps most of all, Allen Rosenberg. These coaches are my heroes. I feed off scraps from their mouths.

I am a remora.

But now I nip at the mouths that feed me.

Back when I was in college we had a expression for any concept so outrageous as to be totally absurd and unthinkable, beyond imagination:

> *"Why, that's like saying 'Fug you!' to the coach!"*
> - anybody on the Penn Lightweight Crew

That's how I feel today! Years ago I started out listening to and studying at the feet of my mentors and heroes. Eventually, I took some of their ideas in some new directions, drew some different conclusions.

Now I find myself actually *disagreeing* with some of their most basic beliefs.

Why, that's like saying fu . . . (You know).

At least that's what it sometimes feels like.

I revere these men and will forever hold them in high esteem. But, I remind myself that these heroes of the previous generation became heroes precisely by standing on the shoulders of the great coaches that preceded *them*.

I owe it to my heroes and to our sport to attempt to find my own way and to share it with others.

And so with some trepidation, I carry on.

Along for the Ride

Allen Rosenberg.

He would never claim to be the originator of the Sequential/Rosenberg Style. After all, he was only codifying what he himself, had been taught.

But, in so doing, he would be overly modest. He certainly was and is the Johnny Appleseed of the Sequential Rowing Style.

Allen Rosenberg, himself, describes his style as follows: "With the feet planted, the sequence of leg drive, back swing and arm draw unfolds using the strongest, next strongest and least strong muscle groups . . . in that overlapping order."

Now that sounds reasonable. Right?

I used to think so, but not any more.

Think hard about it. Again, Rosenberg states that the stroke is "roughly seventy percent legs, twenty percent back and ten percent arms, so the first phase would be your leg drive, and before the legs are totally exhausted, the back is now beginning to move. As the legs phase out, the back comes in. As the back phases out, the arms come in, so there is no finishing point where back, legs and arms are together."

To gain some perspective on the Sequential/Rosenberg Style, I suggest we equate rowing with the discus event.

Yes, the *discus*. Bear with me.

Both events involve complex motions involving the entire body from fingertips to toes with the intent of propelling an object held in the fingers as far as possible through a fluid medium, air having the properties of a liquid at the speed the disc travels.

Am I right or *what?*

The obvious differences are that the discus thrower gets a few tries and is then judged on a single best throw for distance while rowers get judged on around 200 consecutive "throws" of the boat.

166

Think of a rowing event as the summation of 200 efforts to propel the boat for distance.

Oh, and of course the discus thrower propels his disk and then watches its independent flight, while the rower propels his or her boat and goes along for the ride.

Besides that, the two are remarkably similar events.

Now, pause to think about *that* for a moment!

Please.

All right. Now would you suggest that a discus thrower use his muscles sequentially, from strongest to weakest, or weakest to strongest, or any other order? Isn't it more reasonable for the thrower to orchestrate all the various potentials of his body into a natural, proportionate, organic harmony that accelerates the discus to as high a terminal velocity as possible?

And isn't that what in fact they do?

Why wouldn't that also be good advice for rowers? Those immutable laws of physics are the same for both sports.

Think of it another way. Would you recommend to a discus thrower that he begin his throwing motion explosively . . . or would you recommend he bring the discus smoothly up to maximum speed just at the moment it leaves the tips of his fingers?

And isn't that, in fact, what he does?

And isn't that the East German approach to rowing as described by Dr. Koerner? by Dietrich Rose? by Jim Moroney?

Is this a coincidence?

I don't think so.

Can you think of any sport, any human activity, where Rosenberg's advice of sequential muscle application would sound reasonable?

I can't.

The last time I dared to suggest there was an alternative to the Sequential/Rosenberg Style of Rowing, Allen Rosenberg himself absolutely pilloried me in print.

Mercilessly. I was astonished.

I never expected the Spanish Inquisition!

"Nobody expects the Spanish Inquisition!"
- Monty Python's Flying Circus

But it didn't change my mind, and it also didn't change my opinion of what a great man Allen Rosenberg has been for me and for our sport.

He has been a father figure of sorts to me.

For those of you still believing in the Sequential/Rosenberg Style Steve Gladstone suggests you put this book down this very minute and go read Steve Redgrave's book.

For the rest of you, welcome to my world.

A Bill of Goods

For the two or three of you left with an open mind, read on, because here's the most potentially confounding and controversial of all my conclusions.

This will *really* get your dander up!

How you achieve a surging pullthrough is completely counterintuitive. (Where have you heard me say *that* before?) You do it not with the legs, not even with the back, but with the most important group of muscles, the group that requires the most skill from the athlete.

Mallory's Third Law of Hydrodynamics: The real secret to boat moving is right in front of you, it's in your arms. (The "Arm Law.")

Didn't I promise you bass ackwards?

The role of the arms has been the most difficult piece of the puzzle for me, the one I had the most trouble believing, literally the most opposed to my upbringing.

> *"Oh, Popeye!"*
> - Olive Oyl

And yours, too, of course.
And so you see, as the old expression goes:

> *"We have all been sold a bill of goods."*
> - Sumerian clay tablet

But I can assure you I began at least as skeptical as the rest of you are about to be.
You have to remember. I was taught just like the rest of you, rowed just like the rest of you . . . only worse!

* * * * *

169

An interesting thing recently happened to me in the course of writing this book. I handed a copy of the nearly completed manuscript to a civilian co-worker to read. She had seen rowing exactly once in her life at the last San Diego Crew Classic, but intuitively she already knew how to move boats, and she can't understand why my message would be so controversial.

The message of this book makes perfect sense to her because she doesn't know doodley squat about rowing, doesn't have any preconceptions, doesn't have a head full of conventional wisdom.

> *"A child of five would understand this.*
> *. . . (Comedic pause) . . .*
> *Send somebody to fetch a child of five!"*
> — Groucho Marx

* * * * *

Here's food for thought. How many Olympic champions have come from the United States in the last forty years? Answer: not many.

One is my old friend Brad Alan Lewis, who won an Olympic gold medal in the double in 1984. He's a big guy, started his rowing career not quite good enough to make the 1974 UC Irvine Varsity Eight coached by a young Bob Ernst. It was the same year I was coaching at Cal State Long Beach.

You've got to start somewhere!

At the time Bob Ernst didn't know doodley squat about rowing, either. He'd been a water polo coach.

Sound familiar?

Bob didn't know it was uncool for heavyweights to train with lightweights, so his guys and my guys trained together.

And Bob had his guys training in singles and pairs.

Sound familiar?

Bob Ernst didn't know the UC Irvine Anteaters couldn't possibly compete with the University of Washington Huskies. He didn't have a head full of conventional wisdom.

And at the Western Sprints those foolish UCI guys came within one deck of actually beating the unbeatable UDub, who were only undefeated on the West Coast for a generation.

170

(A deck. Five feet? More than a hiccup. Less than a belch.)

People noticed. Now Bob Ernst is Head Coach of the University of Washington.
There *is* a God!

And many of the guys in that UCI program are *still* contributing to the sport.
Not the least of whom is Brad Alan Lewis, JV athlete, Olympic champion sculler, America's Cup grinder, gadfly and published author.
Among his credits are *Assault on Lake Casitas* and *Wanted: Rowing Coach*, both "must-reads" for rowers. And his latest book is about *Baywatch!* A man who lives life to the fullest. Oh yes!

For a quarter century Brad has brought smiles to the Southern California rowing community. The training schedule that my masters four is following in 1989 was formulated by our three man, Glenn Schweighardt, an exercise physiologist, in consultation with none other than Brad Alan Lewis.
Hmm!
But the reason I mention Brad Alan Lewis at this particular juncture, when we are discussing the role of arms in moving boats, is that Brad says he only got fast when he took time out, went to the weight room and put on ten pounds of pure upper body muscle.
Arms. Shoulders.
If you'd told me *that* thirty-five years ago, you know what I would have said?

> *"How could he be so stupid?"*
> - Peter Mallory

Not any more!

* * * * *

And now for the obligatory historical perspective. . .
In 1925, Bourne also wrote, "During the first part of the stroke, when legs, loins, and back are doing all the work, the arms should be perfectly straight . . . Indeed, if the beginning has been well caught, the strain on the arms is such that they are pulled taught, as is a hauser bringing in a

ship to her moorings . . . As the oar comes to lie at right angles to the boat and the wrists pass over the knees, the arms begin to bend home and the stroke enters into its last phase."

In his 1978 FISA presentation Koerner stated, "The arm draw does not get into it until the legs and trunk have overcome the heaviest resistance, that is when the hands are almost to the knees. Drawing in the arms sets up a good finish."
"Drawing in the arms sets up a good finish."
I like that.

In 1982 Canadian National Coach Alan Roaf wrote in the *Canada Rowing 2 Manual*, "The beginning of the stroke is initiated by both the leg drive and the body swing (while) the arms are held straight throughout the first half of the stroke."
"Are held straight?"
Hmm!

All these men are accurately describing the arm motion we have all observed in good rowing, sweep or sculling, small boats to eights. No controversy here, right? So far we are still on the same page. With our own eyes, without still photography or film or videotape or computers or some coach pointing out the obvious, we can clearly see that proper arm *motion* only begins at midstroke.
But were these authors recommending that arm *effort* is also only to begin at midstroke? I can't tell for sure from the quotes. Can you?
Have you ever even asked yourself this question?
Have you? When should you start pulling with the arms?
Midstroke. Right?
Right? Is there even an alternative?

Conventional wisdom says, "No! Absolutely not!"

Let's return to Burnell: "At the catch the arms should be **relaxed**, and straight . . . The arms should begin to flex naturally, about a third of the way through the stroke, and their contribution to the propulsion of the boat follows this, building to a maximum draw at the finish." (My emphasis)
I believe Burnell uses the word "relaxed" to mean there should be no arm effort at the catch, and I submit that he describes well the orthodoxy

that the vast majority of American coaches believe and teach, that the coaches in my own club believe and teach.

Burnell describes well the technique the vast majority of American crews today emulate . . . and implement.

But not everyone.

Not me . . . and I have company.

Listen to Harvard Coach Harry Parker on the subject:

"The basic application of power begins at the moment the bottom edge of the blade touches the water. At that moment all movement toward the stern stops, and movement toward the bow begins. The beginning is very important because all three of the major muscle groups used in rowing must be engaged at that point. **Once the blade drops, the legs, back and arms all engage simultaneously – not in the sequence of one or two and then the third, but all three at the same instant.**" (My emphasis.)

There it is. *Concurrent* power application. Arms at the catch! Back, too, for that matter, *just like me!*

All wrapped up with a pretty ribbon tied into a bow.

(And a darned good description of back splash in the bargain!)

So if you don't believe me, will you at least consider believing Harry Parker?

Is there anyone you respect more than Harry Parker?

Anyone more credible?

Is there?

Out on a Limb Together

Allen Rosenberg, too, has carefully considered the use of arms, and have been privileged to personally debate the subject at length with him in print and in person.

Allen has told me he completely disagrees with me on all aspects of power application.

I don't think so. At least not on arms. While we do hold utterly different views as to the Sequential vs. Concurrent use of legs and back there appears to be only a very subtle distinction between us when it comes to arms.

Not so with the rest of you Burnellians, I must say! I submit to you that Harry Parker and I are out on a limb together. Come join us, Allen. There's plenty of room!

Allen Rosenberg describes his trademark piston-like leg drive at the catch working against a rigid lower back and straight but "alive" arms. "Not relaxed, not actively attempting to bend either."

At the catch, "they're straight but not stiff, as opposed to many other styles, where the arms remain rigid."

Allen continues in his own words, recorded April 6, 1975, in San Diego: "Now what makes one style different from another? Well, it's whether you catch with a stiff arm, whether you catch with a little life in it or a little bend in it, or whether you have a compromise: catch with a stiff and then go to a broken."

That day Allen maintains that everybody who is anybody in the world: the British, East Germans, Russians, New Zealanders all catch with stiff arms . . . everybody but *him*, that is. What did he have his 1974 World Champion Eight do?

"As they lock up, there will be a slight break in the elbow. . . . The reason we do that is to immobilize the upper back."

"How does that immobilize the upper back?" he is asked by a very curious and skeptical listener.

"It destroys the linkage between the arms and back. If your arms are stiff, your back is involved. If your arms are loose, you can't use your back."

174

Other crews "maintain a rigid arm so that the upper body can swing back."

Fascinating . . . I think?

Allen teaches live arms to elicit a counterintuitive result, namely to prevent the back swing from competing with and interfering with his signature explosive leg drive, in the first portion of the stroke.
I'll take his word for it that this actually works in his boats, though I have never tried it.
I'll take his word for it because I believe that the interrelationship between arms, back and legs is organic, mostly subconscious and far more subtle and complicated than most coaches realize.
I'll take his word for it because I think that often in rowing, as in life, you have to *think* one thing in order to *accomplish* another.
I'll take his word for it because I will never need this phenomenon, nor any other that "destroys the linkage" between any parts of the body in rowing. As you probably have surmised, I don't believe in that.
I'll take his word for it because it means all of you skeptics out there have to recognize that a coach renowned worldwide for his intellectual approach to the sport and for his Olympic and world championships, a coach who disagrees with me on almost everything else, nevertheless recognizes the value of live arms at the catch!
However we might otherwise disagree, and my Heavens we *do*, at least Allen Rosenberg and Harry Parker and I all believe that the active involvement of the arms in the first half of the stroke (the portion of the stroke where they don't actually bend) is crucial to the success of the stroke as a totality.
Think about that!

No, I really mean it!

We'll come back to this, I assure you. But right now you're probably *verklempft*. Put this book down for a few minutes, discuss amongst yourselves, and consider the import of my statement . . . of *our* statement. Harry. Allen. Me.
I'm in *excellent* company, don't you think?

A Single Squigiulum

Here's the problem with Mallory's Third Law of Hydrodynamics my Arm Law. And the Second. And the First. With *all* of my laws.

You won't believe me.

You won't believe me if I tell you I have figured all this out on my own in my single. After all, what have I ever won? At best, I had some friends who were truly great.

I have been tremendously ordinary as an athlete, don't you think? have been Patroclus, never Achilles. Rose right to the level of my incompetence. Repeatedly failed when it really counted.

Why listen to me?

So I won't tell you I figured out that delayed arm effort is inefficien through my own rowing. I won't tell you that my research with a loac sensor has revealed that athletes who delay their arm effort have a discontinuity in force application.

"Big deal!" you would say.

"Big deal! Look at the source!"

Instead I'll say, "You don't have to take my word for it. All the information is *already* right in front of you.

"Take it step-by-step."

1. If you delay the arms, the back motion finishes before the arm motion, every time.

    (See the first Burnell quote earlier.

    Try it yourself. Again if you like.)

2. When the back motion finishes early, the boat stops accelerating early, every time.

    (See Mallory's Second Law.

    Try it yourself. The pick drill. Again, if you like.)

Now, forgive my redundancy, let me repeat:

1. If you delay arm effort, the back ends early.
2. If the back ends early, the boat stops accelerating early.
3. Therefore, the rest of the stroke has to be wasted opportunity as far as moving boats in concerned.

And since moving boats is what we're all concerned about, isn't it reasonable to conclude you'll go faster if you don't waste a single squigiulum of the rowing stroke?

Isn't that reasonable?

Welcome to my world!

Welcome Aboard

"If arm effort after the end of back effort in the second half doesn't work," you might ask, "then what *does* work?

"What are you really recommending, Peter, and how do you make it happen?"

Another good question.

Let me summarize.

The moment of initiation of arm effort is an element of style difficult to discern with the naked eye, but I think we can agree that almost all rowers in America have been taught not to attempt arm draw until the second half of the stroke.

There is an alternative. Start pulling from the very instant of entry into the water, just like Harry Parker recommends.

Use the arms from entry to release, just as you use the back from entry to release, just as you use the legs from entry to release.

Concurrent Rowing Style!

The opposite of Sequential. The opposite of the Rosenberg Style.

Bingo! We have another winner! Works in a single. Ask any sculler.

Works in an eight. Go to the Collegiate Nationals. Go to the World Championships. Take a good look.

Look very carefully.

Not everybody, oh my no, not even the majority, often not the winners.

Just the overachievers . . .

Take a *good* look.

Have you ever before taken a really good look? Dietrich Rose did. Thanks to Jim Moroney, I did, too.

Now it's your turn. We pass the baton.

Do you have the courage to run with it?

* * * * *

I have already stated the irony of arm motion. If you actively attempt to pull in with your arms from the catch, and if you are effectively squeezing with the legs and swinging with the back like you're supposed to, then the arms actually move (or don't move) exactly the way Koerner and Rosenberg and you and I and every other coach in the world say they should: They are held more or less straight during the first half of the stroke.

But here's the secret: When you initiate effort from the catch, they almost automatically coordinate with and finish with the back in the second half of the stroke.

(I say *almost* automatically. You are still going to have to coach this nuance, and, like all coaching, it's quite a challenge to do it just right.)

But this is so cool. You look the same . . . and yet there is a fundamental difference. Try it yourself. The only way for the arms and back to finish simultaneously is to have arm effort begin at the catch.

Insight!

Completely counterintuitive!

"But," you might say, "if all you're trying to do is have the arms and back finish the stroke together, why not delay the arms and then just finish the stroke the way you describe? Wouldn't you then have the best of both worlds?"

Read my lips.

"It doesn't work. Can't do it. I don't know why . . . but it can't be done. But don't take my word for it.

"Try it!"

It's just like the fact that a rower can't eliminate boat check and get a properly timed backsplash entry without squaring the blade early. Can't do it.

It's subconscious. Roll up late, you stop your slide in the stern, you hesitate, the boat hesitates, you go in late, you miss water.

Every time.

Years ago I stopped asking why and started telling my crews just to roll up early and their problems would be solved. And it worked.

Every time.

Likewise, I have stopped asking why arm draw from the catch is crucial to a coordinated stroke, a coordinated finish. It just is.

This is hard to accept, I know.

A friend recently posed the following: "If I perform a dead hang on a chin-up bar I can stay up there indefinitely, even with a cox'n hanging on to me.

"But if I tense my arms, raise myself *even one inch*, then my arms tire quite quickly.

"Doesn't that prove that you should 'hang' on the oar in the first half of the stroke?"

No. No it doesn't.

I would be the first to recommend a dead hang if rowing were a dead hang contest, but it's not. And if you have a one inch break in your arms in the first half of the stroke, then you're doing it wrong.

If you catch at full extension, the way you should, no amount of arm effort will yield even one inch of arm draw.

"But," you might say, "isn't it wasted effort to try to bend the arms when everyone can see they can't bend, when they are 'taut as a hauser'? Won't the attempt tire you out?"

Good question. Experience and force graph analysis prove the benefit of early arm effort.

"What counts is the organic whole!"

"That's no answer, Peter. That's *male bovine fecal material!*" you might retort, fury in your voice.

"Just try it!" I might respond, over and over.

Try this: *Change your mindset*. Change your mental conception of what you're trying to accomplish with your oar.

Some people seem to row as if they were a prize fighter trying to knock out their opponents, as if they were boxing with their oars.

Instead, think of those whirlpools or "puddles" created in the water by your oar each stroke. Make it your goal to send those puddles down past the stern of your boat the way you might throw a Frisbee.

180

Better yet, think of your oar as a lacrosse stick and your puddle as the lacrosse ball. Now *send* that lacrosse ball.

WhooooOOOOOSH!

Coordinate your legs, your back and your arms into *sending* your puddle. That's dynamic, organic acceleration. Nothing like a dead hang. Nossirree.

Doesn't sound reasonable to you yet, does it? Good for you! Question it. Try it.

Put down the book and try it.

Seriously.

Even on the ergometer, the flywheel sounds different when you do it right.

WhooooOOOOOSH!

In summary:

If you want to accelerate the boat right up to the instant of release from the water, you have to initiate arm effort immediately at the catch and coordinate the arms, back and legs throughout the stroke so they finish their motions together at the release.

* * * * *

By the way, in discussing this matter at length with Canadian Coach Alan Roaf, quoted earlier, he has assured me he never intended to imply that arm effort should be delayed until the second half of the stroke. So Parker and Rosenberg and Mallory are not entirely alone!

Bravo Alan! Welcome aboard.

Precious Opportunity

Let's go back to the heart of the Sequential/Rosenberg Style.

You're probably thinking, "Hey Peter. Here's a quarter. Go buy a clue!

"As massive as it is, an eight-oared shell requires, nay, *demands* explosive effort to move it effectively!

"I know, Peter. I know of which I speak. I've *been* there!"

"Sure you have," I reply.

"Now go try to push your car with explosive effort. Get a good running start if you like. Go for it. *Explode* into that fender."

Now ask yourself, "Just *how* stupid do I feel?" and get that broken shoulder looked after.

But you might ask, in an eight especially, "Aren't you wasting a precious opportunity by foregoing our traditional explosive leg drive in favor of a sculler's less aggressive leg squeeze?"

> *"They'll call you a sissy . . . "*
> - Monty Python

I love this one. This is the Greg Lahkso conundrum.

National champion Cal Coach Steve Gladstone tells me he runs into this all the time. When he first instructs athletes to forgo explosive legs in favor of surging pullthrough, they accuse him of asking them to pull less hard.

Hah!

HAH!

Here's the answer:

Remember the lacrosse stick. The whole point is to build speed to the end of the stroke. Explosive legs certainly maximize initial power . . . but the effort can't be maintained to the finish.

Just can't.

Don't forget! The whole point is to *maximize* the cumulative result by the finish of the stroke. Get a grip! The whole point is *boat speed*.

Explosive legs don't accomplish that!

And it's not easier. Doing it right is not easier, believe you me!

Your challenge is to put *all* your energy, *all* your intensity, into a reshaped and meatier power curve.

* * * * *

Here's the way it looks on a force graph when a well-coached, world-class athlete rows sequentially:

Biofeedback Engineering

Kind of the way you'd expect, don't you think?

Note the initial spike caused by the explosive application of the legs. Very impressive, don't you think?

Can't match that with a surging pullthrough! Nosirree!

Then comes a second peak as the back heaves over. Again, impressive.

Then a third, lesser peak as the arms make their valiant effort to finish strong.

"Sequential power application is *by definition* a series of discre
pulses, Allen Rosenberg, my dear friend! No amount of overlap ca
overcome the discontinuities, not even with you *personally* coaching, sı
Can't be done! The laws of physics prevent it.

"Ask Professor Brent Rushall of San Diego State. He's an expert
both physics and rowing, and he's done the research."

And all the rest of you experienced rowers already know thi
You've all rowed plenty of times with explosive guys and felt the
explosive leg drive as a discreet event.

An explosion is, by definition, a discreet event! **By definition!**

You can't ask Bill Wark any more . . . but you can certainly as
Chuck Crawford. Surely, *he* will tell you! He's felt *my* discreet event
Oh my, yes!

Tell Chuck I said hello. Tell him I'm in the phone book. Del Ma
California.

You've probably heard the expression "row ugly," maybe even use
it with *pride!* Now you've got to admit that graph on the previous pag
is double-butt ugly! Just look at it!

"And don't tell me you can do any better, Allen. Seriously, I hav
graphed hundreds of athletes, even some of your very own athletes, ar
the graph on this page is the *best* you can hope for! It is what it i
believe you me!"

Bumper Sticker

Now here's the force graph of a real-live well-coached world-class athlete rowing the Concurrent Style, rowing the way I have been trying to describe to you:

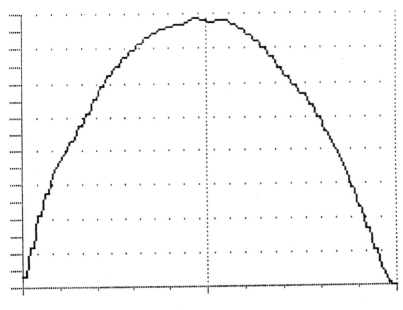

Biofeedback Engineering

Notice the difference!   Isn't it awesome?   organic?   elegant? inspirational?

A parabola!

Who'd a thunk it? Totally unexpected!

> *"A picture is worth a thousand words."*
> - old proverb

185

Isn't your eye intuitively drawn to this curve? Step aside, Allen Rosenberg! The Hand of God drew that second curve.

The Hand of *God!* Simple as that.

> *"Send somebody to fetch a child of five!"*
> - Groucho Marx

Incidentally, there is more area underneath the second curve, and, as even agnostic calculusians well know, more area under the curve equals more work done.

More work!

More boat speed!

Don't believe me? Make copies of the two curves and overlay them.

Now do you believe me?

Fill a two-dimensional sack with two-dimensional water, and guess what shape it takes, guess what shape maximizes the area of a two-dimensional sack?

A parabola, for Heaven's sake . . . literally.

A parabola!

For Heaven's sake!!!!!!

There's the proof.

God is a rower, and He rows like *me!*

Game. Set. Match to the curmudgeonly prick of misery from Del Mar, California.

AND you are building organically from catch to release in a manner that maximizes return for your efforts in a water environment. Quack.

BUT since you are accelerating the boat the *entire* pullthrough instead of just the first quarter . . . or the first half . . . or even the first three quarters, since you are being more effective, since you are doing more work, you *will* get tired at first.

186

"You must fully understand that strength and conditioning are at least eighty-five percent of the process!" So says Steve Gladstone.

Here's a suggestion for a bumper sticker:

"You Have to Train Like the Devil to Row Like God!"
- Peter Mallory

Believe you me, pardner.
And they called you a sissy.

Steve and I laugh out loud!

Sorry

"But," you might still ask, "but isn't explosive leg drive unused the equivalent of explosive leg drive wasted? Isn't that foregone effort lost forever?"

No.

No, it isn't.

During the course of the race your body intuitively marshals its potentials to deal with the challenges at hand, no matter what they may be. Effort not expended on legs is channeled to the back, to the arms, to the lungs, to wherever it is most needed.

Let us continue the music analogy. There is a processing function within your body like a record producer changing the mix of the various instruments in order to arrive at the most harmonious result from the materials available. In your body the result is an exhausted total organism at the end of the race, not a segmented athlete with some heavily utilized and therefore overtired muscles but underutilized and therefore fresh legs.

Has anybody, even someone rowing the way I recommend, ever finished a race with fresh legs?

I don't think so. Never heard of such a silly thing.

And don't forget my rubber ducky. Punch the water, and the water sneers back in derision. Surge through, and the water bends to your will.

Ever since the days of Karl Adam and Ratzeburg Rowing Club the great eights, the national composite teams, now even the successful American collegiate varsities, they all train off-season in small boats, train in pairs.

Have you ever asked yourself why?

I always assumed it was to develop better balance, but that's stupid. What national eight was ever held back by its inability to balance their boat?

Maybe it never occurred to their coaches. It certainly never occurred to *me* that these athletes training in pairs might be unconsciously, even accidentally, *despite* their coach's best efforts, in fact, by trial-and-error learning what moves boats and what doesn't.

188

Maybe they are developing a "small boat touch . . . "
Dare I say it?
" . . . a sculler's touch?"
And maybe *that's* what makes them fast in eights.
Hmm!

"But," you might bring up, "now that training methods have advanced to the point that ratings are up to 38, 39, even 40, there's no time for back swing, no time for layback, no time to finish with the arms, so all you've got left is legs. They're the only muscles that can react fast enough.

"You have to pound the catch to get anything at all done before the stroke is over!"

You know, it's true boats today are nine or ten percent faster than in my youth, so the oar must be traveling through the water nine or ten percent faster, right? That's also about the increase in strokes per minute, so it's reasonable to conclude that not just pullthrough, the time spent *in* the water, but also recovery, the time spent *out* of the water, has decreased by nine or ten percent.

So the tempo has increased as athletes have become more fit, but rhythm and ratio have remained more or less the same. Good rowing is still good rowing. At 34. At 44.

And everything in between.

And the arms and back are still required to make good music. Oh yes.

All my laws, all of God's immutable laws, still apply. "Train like the Devil." A parabola's still a parabola.

Sorry.

Don't believe it can be done at high rating in an eight? Take a good look at a video of the 1999 Cal Varsity, a legitimate 5:32 crew made up of college undergraduates.

Rowing parabolas.

I rest my case.

* * * * *

Interesting thing about higher ratings. It's nothing new, you know. Scullers have been doing it for generations.

Back in 1973 after the Nationals, when we were selecting our lightweight candidates for the National Camp in Dartmouth, we ran whole bunch of guys through the two Australian ergometers at the Penn Boathouse. These machines were among the very first in the country, and most athletes had never sat on one before.

When we were just about finished with the "real" camp candidates who should come up and ask to try just for fun but Bill Belden, just one year shy of his world championship in the lightweight single, along with his double partner, Fred Duling.

I, of course, said, "Go for it!"

I was curious.

* * * * *

Now I've told you primitive ergometer machines are cumbersome affairs. There is one for port rowers, one for starboards, and nobody really knows how to row them yet. It's 1973, for Heaven's sake!

Everybody seems to go at their own pace, paying no attention to the fellow on the other erg right next to them, and most guys end up around 31 or 32 strokes per minute after going like Hell for a couple of minutes and gradually fading every minute thereafter.

Bill and Fred start out at 39 strokes per minute, just swinging away in perfect unison, rowing easily stroke-for-stroke.

They don't look like they're pulling that hard. They don't make a lot of noise, sort of like Larry Wittig in that respect, and while their scores for the first minute or two aren't as high as some of the studs who have preceded them, they don't fade. They just motor to the end. Thirty-nine strokes per minute.

And their overall scores are *excellent!*

They have a completely different approach to power application: less effort on each individual stroke, but more strokes, higher rating. They pace themselves. And they're smooooooth.

Sound familiar?

* * * * *

190

You know, come to think of it, during my Undine summer of 1966, the summer of my four Canadian Henley championships, the summer when only a crab stood between me and a U.S. championship, during that whole summer our base rating was 38 in a four!

We'd overstroke everybody by four or five beats!

Everybody!

Well, at that rating we *couldn't* hit any individual stroke that hard, and so it felt almost like three-quarter pressure muscular effort while we were breathing like freight trains.

The disadvantage seemed to be that the harder-hitting crews would leave us behind at the start. But we would get comfortable, row even splits down the course and roar by most everybody by the end.

Interesting.

Felt great!

"Incidentally, Pete, that's the way my Cal crews row their races today," interjects Steve Gladstone.

Hmm!

Now, back in 1966, nobody told us to row that high in a four. It just felt right that summer.

I'll tell you a secret. That summer Undine got a gorgeous new set of Ayling oars from England with adjustable collars and shovel blades, the product of the revolution in technology brought about by Karl Adam. I don't think our coach, Fred Leonard, had yet figured out how to adjust the leverage of those oars. After all, they didn't come with instructions, and nobody in America had ever adjusted an oar collar before.

Anyway, in the intervening years I have come up with the theory that the collars must have been assembled on those oars by accident in such a way as to make us *feel* like we couldn't get much done on each stroke, like we didn't have much leverage, like we were eating with teaspoons instead of tablespoons, so naturally we had to take more bites!

However it happened, we rowed 38 down the course whenever we used those oars, and even on our less-than-perfect days, the only crew to beat us all summer . . . was *ourselves!*

Very interesting!

* * * * *

I have one more high-stroke story.

I have rowed in a double exactly once with a true world-best sculler.

That first fall of mine in Long Beach, all of us LBRA scullers decid
just for fun to enter several boats in the Mixed Double, you know, on
male with one female, in the Head of the Harbor Regatta over in Sa
Pedro. We draw lots . . . and I draw Joan Lind.

Pinch me.

Well, we get to practice just one afternoon before Coach Tom
McKibbon changes his mind and puts the kybosh on all our reindee
games.

But what an afternoon!

I suggest that Joan stroke our boat, I'll row bow and follow her lead
Well, from the second we leave the dock I feel like I'm on *Mr. Toad'*
Wild Ride! We seem to *paddle* at 38 strokes per minute, and when w
start to put the pressure on . . . well, I have never experienced anything
quite like it . . . before or since.

A rush of sensory input.

* * * * *

Now Joan was and still is a cardiovascular marvel, but as a man
was much stronger than she was. She compensated for the fact that she
could not apply as much power on any individual stroke as I could by
overwhelming her opponents *(and me, her double partner!)* with strokes
that moved the boat all the way to the finish and came in dizzying
succession.

The boat just flew!

But I was completely overwhelmed, my mind overloaded.

And it wasn't just my mind! I was gassed! Proof again that rowing
a surging style is much harder rather than much easier than explosive
rowing.

Mark my words!

By the time we got back to the dock I was terribly embarrassed.
prayed I could complete the adjustment by the next day.

* * * * *

Our next day never came, but I never got over the sensation of
rowing with Joan Lind.

In all my coaching after that day in 1973, I never fully integrated that
experience with Joan into my rowing philosophy.
Unfinished business.
Perhaps I can pass it on to my son one of these days.

Catch-22

Back to the Concurrent Style. Back to Joan Lind's style.
Back to God's style.
You know you're rowing right when the leg, back and arm efforts start together right at the catch, and when leg, back and arm motions finish together with a rush at the release. And that's very hard to achieve.
Worth the effort, though.

"Why?" you might ask. "Why is it worth the effort?"

The basis of every advertisement is a "credible promise," or so I learned in MBA school.
"What are *you* promising, Peter?
"And are you credible?" you might ask, skepticism dripping from your every word.
"A lot . . . and not very," I might reply sheepishly.

Catch-22.
Even after all you have read, even now, nobody will believe me until I deliver proof, and there will be no proof until people believe me.
Rest in peace, Joseph Heller. I can't.

A Stranger in a Strange Land

So, if Joan Lind herself, if God Himself (or Herself) is not enough to convince you, let me continue to enlist other credible earthly spokespersons in my valiant effort to shore up my own credibility.

Let me quote world and Olympic doubles champion Melch Burgin from Switzerland:

"The drive should be increased progressively so that you have your boat at maximum speed at the end of a drive . . . I compare the stroke in rowing with a very heavy door which you don't close from the beginning with all your force, but with always progressively more . . . The oarsman should try to make a hard finish which is very good for the speed of the boat."

Push a car. Close a door. Same idea. Same immutable laws.

Now for those of you who have taken physics, I suggest to you that Melch is confusing the concepts of force and velocity. Ideal power application in rowing comes from constant force yielding constant acceleration yielding constantly increasing *velocity* from catch to release.

(Study note: Highlight that last sentence.)

As you apply constant force to Melch's heavy door (or to your car), it slowly, then smoothly, picks up speed according to a parabolic curve, reaching peak velocity at the moment you stop pushing.

Like a rocket at first slowly, painfully slowly lifting off the pad, then smoothly increasing in speed as it clears the gantry. And up and up into space, accelerating as long as the rocket engine burns.

Or the shot put motion, from initiation to release of the shot.

Or the discus motion, if you think about it.

But this is quibbling.

Melch has it straight in his heart, in the seat of his pants, so to speak.

From the athlete's point of view, even though actual effort should be constant, as the pullthrough gathers speed it takes more and more **perceived** effort, and more and more skill, to maintain acceleration all the way to the end of the stroke. The result is: entry, faster, Faster, FASTER, release.

VrroooOOOOOOM!

Now I'm sure most of you are still resisting, still thinking to yourselves, "Oh sure, all this may be true in a single, but I keep coming back to the same thing. I still just can't believe it's not a different world in an eight. All my experience tells me different. Years of experience! Decades, for Heaven's sake!

"What you say just doesn't sound right, Peter. Things happen faster in an eight. The leverage is different. There's more mass to move. You need to be more forceful, more aggressive.

"Apply your own Reasonableness Principle, Peter!"

I salute you. Your continued skepticism is healthy. A good first step.

Melch was *also* unsure.

In 1970 he stated, "I believe if a four rows this technique it won't be slow because this technique is not exclusively a sculling technique. I am not sure if this technique works in an eight. Which technique the quad should row, I don't know, but I believe that also here you will not find big differences."

Just like you, Melch was speculating that as mass and hull speed increase in quads and especially eights, the fastest events in rowing, perhaps a different force application strategy might indeed be required.

This is the conventional wisdom in America, and not just America, I should point out. As I mentioned, Melch is from Switzerland. Go visit him. He runs *Stämpfli Bootswerft* now. He's the man who taught me how to put a grip on an oar while I was out standing in my field. Perhaps he will teach you, too.

* * * * *

To Melch Burgin I say, "Fear not! Good rowing is good rowing in any boat at any speed, even in an eight!"

Even in an eight!!!!!

It just takes more skill to apply surging power at such lofty velocities.

More skill.

Are you up to the challenge?

Are you?

Go watch a film of Melch's 1968 Swiss double or the Landvoigt pair or the Hansen double. Then watch the great East German fours and eights of the 70s. Sure these latter crews were on steroids, but they were also gorgeously efficient rowers.
"With a sculler's touch," people would say.
"A sculler's touch."
Hmm!

But be careful. I am preaching heresy here. Anyone who questions explosive power application, who questions this bedrock tenet of basic Sequential Rowing, someone like me for instance, or Melch, or Steve Gladstone, or maybe some of you after you read a few more pages, such a heretic risks ridicule and isolation, risks being treated like a stranger in a strange land.
Believe you me, I know.

> *"My ways are not your ways."*
> - John the Baptist

And you know what they did to *him*!

Look into your own heart. Right now.
Be honest.
Don't you, deep down, *still* believe I'm completely full of crap?

Your funeral.

Into Your Noggins

Today, as I sit and write these words in Del Mar, California, as I look back on this life of mine from the perspective of rapidly advancing age, my own fifteen-year-old son Philip, who rows beautifully, just beautifully, just like I taught him, is attending a rowing camp at the Naval Academy in Annapolis, Maryland.

He called last night. His coach there, Dale Hurley, a fine fellow and five-time National Lightweight Team member, world bronze medalist, Royal Henley winner, way ahead of me in the credentials race, in the credibility race, I think we can all agree, and a nice fellow, too, I met him a couple of months ago at the San Diego Crew Classic, Dale told my son that he "looks like a sculler" and will have to be more explosive if he ever wants to be successful in an eight.

"Dale, take another look at the stroke man of your 2000 Naval Academy Lightweight Varsity. He rows beautifully. Better than *anybody* in the Harvard or Yale boats that beat you at the Crew Classic this year!

"He's beautiful. And he looks like a sculler to me."

* * * * *

In 1985 there was an article published in the American federation's magazine of the era, an article titled "Converting from Sweep Rowing to Sculling" by Anne E. Taubes Warner, a notable and respected sculler. The article treats as self-evident the contention that what works in a slower sculling boat doesn't work in faster sweep boats, and vice-versa:

In sculling "there is more of a sense of accelerating the boat through the water. Some scullers describe it as a 'slower' power application, gradually accelerating the boat through the water. [Athlete A] describes the power application as slightly slower and more gradual with more acceleration to the finish.' In sweep rowing, there is more of an all out explosion at the catch."

* * * * *

198

To Anne Warner, to Dale Hurley, to all you Rosenbergers, to all of you who pound the catch in eights as you were told you must, to all of you who have found a modicum or even a bushel basket-full of success pounding the catch in eights, to all of you who never allowed an original thought into your noggins, to you I say,

"Pish posh! Don't take my word for it. Open your minds, and try it yourself!"

Now You Know

I rest my case. Now you know how to move boats.

Guilty as Charged

Or still you don't get it, still you don't believe me. Why am I not surprised?

To you I say, "Hold tight to your truths! Keep your minds closed!

"It's so . . . *American!*"

> *"I know of no country in which there is so little*
> *independence of mind and real freedom of*
> *discussion as in America."*
>   - Alexis de Tocqueville

(My wife, my pair partner in life but not in boats, thank Heavens, my dear wife, Jeni, tells me that right about here in my book I sound like a fatuous, flap-jawed fussbudget!

Now those certainly aren't the words she uses, oh my no, not the words she would *ever* use, not even close.
Heaven knows, she's much more of a lady than that!
But surely that's what she means.

"GUILTY AS CHARGED, YOUR HONOR!")

The Sirens Call

I am a tortured soul. I must write fast, for there is madness within me.

I am Van Gogh at Arles. I paint in a panic. Broad strokes, bright palette. The night sky is a raging river of stars.

The Sirens call. "Who will bind me to the mast?"

Don't let anybody tell you different. Explosive rowing is for nincompoops! All that work, all that energy, and for what?
For wasted effort? Come on!

Here I finally have the answer, after traveling to the end of the universe and back, traveling for most of my life, and nobody cares, nobody wants to listen.

Run it up the flagpole!
Here it is. Here's the answer:
"Forty-two!"

Salute, dammit!

Boats Rowing Crappy

Not satisfied? Not convinced?
Good for you!
Let's go on. Obviously my passion is not quenched!
The passion of Plutarch and Lewis Carroll, of Homer and Soupy
Sales.
My odyssey not quite complete!

Am I suggesting it's impossible to succeed if you attack the catch?
Or row in any number of other bizarre manners? Of course not! Get big
enough guys, strong enough guys (or gals) all blasting away in unison,
and the boat will respond, however reluctantly, and you'll beat lots of
other boats, even some rowing just beautifully.
Maybe you'll even beat absolutely everybody on a given day.

> *"Different strokes for different folks."*
> - Sly Stone

It's been done before, you know, lots of times. Over the years most
World Championships have been won by boats rowing crappy.
And I'm not exaggerating!
When I finally got to my first World Championships, it blew me
away. Almost everybody rows just terribly! Oh yeah, strong and fit to
be sure. Just terrible style.
Absolutely *frightful* technique!

Even at the Worlds!

Oh, there are a few guys in Great Britain and Australia rowing well.
The training center at Piediluco in Italy turns out some gorgeous quads
and fours, many of them lightweight, and there have been Danish
lightweight fours to die for over the years.
There's a coach in Belgrade today that does it *all.*
And, years after he moved on, here and there you can still see the
good works of Thor Nielsen.
Other than that . . .

Did you know that a good case can be made that the twentieth century's most justifiably famous crew is the 1960 West German Olympic Champion Cox Four, the Bulls of Constance, *die Bodensee Bullen?*

You just *have* to find a film of these guys. They ought to post it on the USRA website for all to see! You won't believe your eyes. They row absolutely *dreadfully!*

They are *bulls*, absolutely true to their names!

> *"Bulls in a china shop."*
> - old proverb

But, oh my Heavens, are they ever big and strong and aggressive!
So there!

And remember, it's also quite possible to row very well, in fact superbly, with a less than perfectly efficient style . . . or with no style at all!

Local races, traditional rivalries, regional championships, national championships, even world championships are often won by extraordinary boats rowing very, very well with a style much, much less efficient than mine (God's), and they get away with it.

Need I remind you that Allen Rosenberg twice guided to the top of the world eights rowing sequentially?

Sequentially!

The top of the world!

Remember, no style points in rowing. It's still eighty-five percent strength and conditioning.

> *"Strength and conditioning will get you lengths and lengths. Technique will get you inches."*
> - Karl Adam, my hero

And, don't forget, at least two of the last century's most continuously successful American collegiate programs have based their success on great big guys rowing badly together.

Everybody knows who they are. And we respect them. And they deserve our respect.

But don't forget. You can't improve on a parabola. Theoretically impossible.

We can argue back and forth . . . we can agree to disagree . . . about who is the better coach, about who makes the best Philly cheese steak, about whether your girl is prettier than mine, and on and on, in all phases of life.

But not about a parabola. A more effective power curve has never been conceived, not even in the mind of God! Ignore that fact in a boat . . . and you sell yourself short by three or four percent!

"The last three or four percent. That's what technique gives you," says Steve Gladstone.

"And that's the difference!" I hasten to add.

"Exactly," says Steve Gladstone. "For me, the difference between winning eight IRA national titles in a career . . . and winning none at all!"

Look at yourself in the mirror.

Can you afford to be wasteful of your own potential? Do you have that much talent to spare? Are you really that good?

Are you really that much better than everybody else?

Ted Nash was in 1960 . . . but not quite in 1964, bronze medal by a hiccup, you may recall.

(*He* recalls, you can bet on that!)

Pete Maxon was that much better in 1972 . . . but no way in 1973. Not even close.

These are tragedies, to be sure.

And remember, these are *giants* in our sport. Giants in life, for that matter!

Are *you* a giant?

I never was. I mean that much better than everybody else. Not me.

But still I might have accomplished great things. Great things. Might have.

I was *that* close . . .

But not the way I was rowing. Another tragedy. Admittedly a small one. No tears for me.

But might you not be another tragedy in the making, another "—, only?"

Someday, when you are an old fart like those guys in blazers a Undine, when you are an old, faded newspaper clipping like me, will yo look back on a career of almosts? Couldas? Shouldas? Mightas?

Like me?

It's your choice.

The Gates of Paradise

Old story:

Three rowers die in a car crash, and they find themselves at the Gates of Paradise. Before entering, they are each asked a question by St. Peter himself.

"When you are in your casket and friends and family and teammates are mourning over you, what would you like to hear them say?"

The first guy ponders a moment with his fist supporting his chin and then confidently replies, "I would like to hear them say . . . that I really attacked the catch, and it was exciting to row with me."

The second guy puts down *this very book* and muses thoughtfully, "I would like to hear them say . . . that I really moved boats, and it was a pleasure to row with me."

The last guy replies, "I would like to hear them say . . . LOOK!!! HE'S MOVING!!!!!"

Sliding Seats

With this book I challenge you, and doesn't my challenge intrigu
you?

Even if you don't need to, even if you're already a world champion
doesn't it just make you salivate to even imagine it might be possible t
take your technique to a higher level?

To a level more subtle, more sophisticated, more challenging, mor
effective?

Good as you already are, wouldn't you *love* to be more efficient?

Apparently not. Ted Washburn, the Harvard Freshman Coach for al
the great Harvard crews in my lifetime, recently opined that mos
coaches have neither the interest nor the patience to pursue technique.

Apparently, Ted Washburn is an extremely cynical man!

Is Ted Washburn describing you? Seriously. In your mind does
there even exist such a concept as "good enough"?

Read Herodotus. Isn't that why the Greeks invented sliding seats?

Good thing they did, too. The world today would look a great dea
different if the Persian Navy hadn't been defeated at the Battle o
Salamis by Greek triremes with sliding seats.

The first true World Rowing Championships.

Only two places in *that* race, pardner!

Strength of Will

Remember my grey-eyed goddess and erstwhile double partner, Joan Lind? At the Olympics in Montreal in 1976, she was the best single sculler there, the *best in the world*, no question about it . . . . but she came in second to a particular East German named Christine Scheiblich who had simply *appalling* technique.

Christine got away with it. She was *that* fast. That much faster than Joan . . . and that much faster than everybody else.

She was that much bigger and stronger, and however we may grumble about how Christine got that way as part of the East German sports machine, still there's no asterisk for "bad style" behind her name on the list of Olympic champions.

Interestingly enough, that's not the end of the Olympic story for Joan Lind. She earned a second Olympic silver in Los Angeles in 1984, this time in a cox quad, but this time with Joan on the other side of the technique fence.

This was my cox'n Kelly Rickon's boat, and her crew was a collection of the flower of American single sculling of that era, Anne Marden in bow, Lisa Rhode in two, Joan in three, and Ginny Gilder in the stroke seat.

Each of them had trained in a single and had been right in the thick of the U.S. Olympic Single Trials, won narrowly by Carly Geer. Then they only had a few weeks to adapt from a single to a quad, and that, as it was every year for American composite crews, that was no mean task.

They rowed that quad with magnificent power and courage, but, not that surprisingly, they just didn't row very well together. One athlete, Ann Marden to be specific, was completely out of sync down the course, completely different body mechanics, and late entering the water every stroke.

Was she the right person for the job? How good was Ann Marden? Silver in the single at the 1988 Olympics, fourth in the single at the 1992 Olympics.

That good!

But a bit of a hammer. Always was. Famous for it.

And the morning of the quad final she woke up with a bad back, which she appeared to be favoring during the race.

So if the boat couldn't move together . . . Ann and the others made up for it by sheer strength of will.

Very American!

And they only lost by half a length.

My admiration knows no bounds!

Half a length to Romania, who rowed just beautifully together. Looked like they had rowed that quad for years instead of weeks, like us.

And you know what? They *had!*

But it's hard not to speculate what might have been, what might have happened if we could have molded our four magnificent individuals, who had so distinguished themselves as single scullers, if we could have molded them into a unified boat.

After all . . . half a length . . .

But to Kelly, Ann, Lisa, Joan and Ginny and to John Van Blom, your coach, I say,

"Bravo! I salute you!"

Maybe That's Why

Question: *"How do you tell the sex of a chromosome?"*
Answer: *"Pull down its genes."*

You might remember from biology that women have two x chromosomes while men, instead, have an x and a y. Someone once pointed out that the x chromosome looks like a oarlock.
Maybe that's why women make such good scullers.

"Life is a metaphor for rowing."
- Peter Mallory

They say the secret to life is locked up in our genes. Perhaps the secret to rowing is there, too.
So if you don't find the answers to your questions in this book, you might find them in the Human Genome Project.
Concentrate your search on the x chromosome. Maybe there's a boat-moving gene. If there is, you can bet Joan Lind has a copy.
And I don't.

* * * * *

While we're on the subject, what ever happened to Joan Lind and me? Joan was the first female I ever met who did the things I respected in my male friends, and did them better than I could. On any given day she often beat me in a single, and in so doing, she taught me a basic truth about life, and in my life I never looked at any woman quite the same again.

Until today I never found the opportunity to tell her.
"Thank you, Joan. I am still learning from your example."

* * * * *

Quick rewind. The night before she leaves for Moscow in 1973 I take Joan Lind to dinner, kiss her on the cheek good night, go home and melt. Three weeks later, she returns home from the Worlds, and my Athena has found her Apollo, John Van Blom.

Of course!

It was so *obvious!*
Could there ever have been a better choice?
I don't think so.

Now, decades later, they're still together, American Rowing's royal family.

Bravo John and Joan and John, Jr.

art credit: John Dawson

(Joan's an authentic hero. I got within zero degrees of separation from Joan Lind!)

His First Hurrah

There's something very American about going about a task with force instead of finesse.

Ulysses Grant won the Civil War for the North with his willingness to throw troops at his Southern opponents and accept staggering levels of human casualties. Harry Truman ended World War II with not one *but two* atomic bombs. We drive big, stupid cars with big, stupid V-8s instead of sleek, efficient foreign cars.

What other country would watch American football or the World Wrestling Federation?

I ask you.

It is no surprise that American rowers also respect force over finesse, respect the Conn Finleys more than the Duvall Hechts?

Is there a single boathouse in our country where lightweights don't take a back seat to heavyweights in prestige, equipment, budget, locker room space?

Were it not for Title IX, which has made women's crew a scam for big football universities to continue to exploit male athletes and placate rabid alumni, were it not for Title IX, where would woman collegiate rowers be today?

> *" . . . barefoot and pregnant!"*
> - of obscure origin

That's where!

Is it any wonder that the prize for the rowing ergometer world championship at the *very* American CRASH-B Sprints every year is a hammer?

A hammer!

Is it any wonder we make American rowing heroes out of our athletes who row like beasts of the jungle?

One of the century's most memorable individual American rowing personalities is our men's Olympic single sculler from Montreal in 1976 (with Joan Lind on the team and with Sy and Gail Cromwell and me in the grandstands). His name is Jim Dietz.

Six feet, six inches, 200 pounds. Huge guy, kind of a high voice, always laughing, always a smile on his face, always a story to tell. Just about the most gregarious guy ever to pick up an oar.

I always thought Jim's body mechanics were better than average, but in his approach to force application, well, he was hardly subtle.

Nevertheless, I think he's won more U.S. and Canadian championships than anyone in history.

And Jim Dietz was the first man ever to break seven minutes for 2,000 meters in a single, rowing in flat water.

So there!

art credit: John Dawson

The picture above is based on a famous photo of Jim taken the day he set his world record in Lucerne, Switzerland. We see him in mid-stroke, his head thrown back, his face distorted in pain, every muscle striving to get that last ounce of effort into his oars.

Look at that picture and you might conclude Jim Dietz rows a boat the same way Elvis Presley left this Earth:

> *"Cause of Death: Straining at stool."*
> - Coroner's Report

214

But, when I look at the picture a second time, I can also see the exact opposite. I see a man, eyes closed, his head raised to the Heavens as if he were listening to a voice only he could hear, to some divine revelation, his face distorted in ecstasy.

I see a martyred saint in a religious painting. All he needs is a bunch of arrows stuck in his body.

But sitting in the stands in Montreal, I can tell you Jim Dietz reminds me not of Elvis Presley . . . nor of St. Sebastian . . . but of James Brown, the Godfather of Soul.

You know, all these years after I sat in the stands, that one race is the only one I really remember in any detail from Montreal. Not Joan's single race, not the women's eight with my own cox'n Lynn Silliman (and with Anita de Frantz in seven), not Allen Rosenberg's men's eight, just the men's single.

At the front of the pack Perrti Karpinnen, a giant fireman from Finland, 6'8" and 230 pounds, was beating Peter Michael Kolbe, a young and supremely gifted West German, a mere 6'5" and 200.

Kolbe had gambled, gone out strong and taken the early lead. Karpinnen rowed through him, and then Kolbe just packed it in, actually giving up with 300 meters to go.

Only two places in that race for Peter Michael Kolbe!

I remember because it astonished me that Kolbe could have been *that good* . . . and not had the courage or the class to finish the race with the whole world watching.

But I was even more fascinated by Jim Dietz. His first 500 was prodigious, but he'd made it look so much harder than Karpinnen.

Perrti Karpinnen rowed high for such a massive guy, and he was deceptively smooth, a sculler's sculler. And, by the way, he rowed parabolas. Check it out for yourself on the cover of *Rudersport,* May 9, 1986.

By contrast, Jim rowed explosively.

Sound familiar?

Now I have a theory about pacing in races. It seems to be that sometimes there is a correlation between how a person rows a single stroke and how that same person tends to row an entire race. One is a metaphor for the other.

Anyway, just as he exploded the first quarter of every stroke, Jim Dietz exploded the first quarter of his 1976 Olympic final, but, just like a Rosenberger can't maintain an explosive catch all the way to the end of the stroke, poor Jim couldn't keep up his initial pace all the way to the end of the race.

Through the middle of the course, Jim went slower and slower and was passed by one after another of his competitors. Looking more and more dejected, Jim looked like the Energizer Bunny with his batteries finally running down.

Ever been to a James Brown concert? There's a good reason why they call James Brown "the Hardest Working Man in Show Business."

It's because he really *is* the hardest working man in show business.

He works himself into such a lather that he runs out of steam, he slumps over the microphone. You think he might pass out at any second. The band slows down, the crowd despairs.

Finally, and not a moment too soon, members of the Famous Flames appear from the wings, envelope their leader and mentor in a silken cape, and support him on either side as he staggers away from center stage . . .

The band has slowed the beat to a . . . dirge - like . . . cadence . . .

And then suddenly, James Brown awakens from his stupor, breaks free from his handlers, tosses his cape aside and rushes back to the microphone and begins another, even *more* frenetic chorus of "I Feel Good!" to the thunderous applause of the crowd!

Well, as Jim Dietz enters the last few hundred meters of the Olympic Singles final, somehow he finds renewed inspiration from somewhere. Suddenly he tosses aside his imaginary cape and comes storming back on the field.

"The Hardest Working Man in Row Business."

"The Godfather of Row."

Of course, it was too little, too late, but still I was mesmerized!

I kept wondering how well he might have done if he had rowed his race more consistently.

Of course, I also kept wondering how well he might have done had he rowed each *stroke* more consistently . . .

. . . if he had surged!

But that was not Jim Dietz, never had been. All the way back to the beginning of his rowing career, he was a man raging against the world.

I can tell you this, because I was there at Jim's very first race.

* * * * *

1965 inaugural Head of the Charles. It's Friday, with evening coming on, cloudy, windy, getting dark, and I'm going over the winding river course in Cambridge for the first time in my life.

I'm scared as Hell. My first single race.

First one.

Hell of a place to start. All those bridges . . . all those turns . . . even buoys, and the water is rough as the dickens tonight.

From out of the gloom comes this enormous gangly fourteen-year-old kid from New York A.C., talkingamileaminute in a Bronx accent all about how he loves the rough water, hopes it is rougher still during the race, how he loves to pound away at the elements, actually praying for rain and cold, too.

"The worse the better!" declares Jimmy Dietz.

"What an asshole!" I think to myself, praying just as hard for mirror-smooth conditions.

Despite Jim's exhortations, the next day turns out gorgeous, I come in second in my junior lightweight single race, beaten by seven seconds by a fellow named Lee Chu from Choate, never met him, but I've been haunted ever since by that alliteration . . . and Jim Dietz overcomes the good weather to win the junior heavyweight single race.

* * * * *

His first hurrah.

I Doubt It

One of Jim Dietz's last hurrahs as an oarsman found him in 1984 teamed with the most famous hammer of my lifetime, Tiff Wood.

Compared to Tiff Wood, Jim Dietz was a *stylist!*

Tiff was (and still is) a slight fellow for a heavyweight rower, maybe 180 pounds, always seems to have a slightly embarrassed look on his face, did his rowing at St. Paul's and Harvard.
Dietz towered over Tiff Wood in 1984.
He still does.

But these two men went nowhere when they most needed to. They didn't make the 1984 Olympic Team, a true tragedy.
Jim is the author of the "killing fish" quote I used earlier, and he said it to Tiff as they were trying to put a winning double together.
Trying unsuccessfully, I should add.
You can read all about it in *The Amateurs* by David Halberstam, the best book about rowing since *Jason and the Argonauts* and *Men Against the Sea.*
Halberstam has made Tiff Wood into a genuine legend, a figure of literature as well as flesh and blood, a tragic hero . . . and the poster child for attacking the water in a shell.

Tiff is also a personal hero of mine. I always imagined that he had Pete Mallory's Disease, but with a difference.
According to Halberstam: "Wood was able to waste immense amounts of energy with poor technique and still succeed."
I couldn't. Tiff Wood was just plain better than me.
That much better.
Another giant in our sport.
Lucky guy . . .

Even in prep school Tiff had a reputation as a thug in a boat . . . and he *reveled* in it. In his own words: "It always used to amuse me. How could I possibly be a hammer when I was the smallest guy in the boat?
"But if people wanted to *consider* me a brute, well . . . "

218

Listen to *this*, again from *The Amateurs:* "When he drove his oars into the water, he did it with such fury and strength that it virtually drove a physical shock into his body."

I *love* this man!

That was *me!* I was the lightweight version, anyway.

"His instinct, when something went wrong, was simply to pull harder, to punish himself a little more. . . On some days he thought he was rowing so well that he could move a boat all by himself."

Again, that was *me!*

At least until I learned better, and I mean that with all humility.

But it should come as no surprise to the reader to learn that I have evolved beyond my own original heavy-handed approach and attitude, that now I respectfully disagree with my good friend Tiff Wood.

What did I learn? What is my new philosophy?

> *"I want you to remember that no bastard ever won a war*
> *by dying for his country. He won it by making the other*
> *poor dumb bastard die for his country."*
> - General George Patton, United States Army

"What's that got to do with rowing, Pete?" you might ask.

Let me explain.

My rowing version of the Patton credo: In a shell, don't try to win the race by yourself, try to get your teammates to win the race *for you.*

Now what do we mean by that?

I mean that nobody can win by himself or herself, not even Tiff Wood, I venture to suggest. But if you row in such a way as to make the boat more congenial for your teammates, with better set, better surge, better swing, smoother in all ways, if you aspire to make the boat work for your teammates, if you pull through not to get *your* oars through the water but to help your teammates get *their* oars through the water, then all of them will be more comfortable, more enthused and more effective, and your positive input will be magnified and multiplied as it is channeled through them.

Now imagine each of your teammates also having the same mind-set and trying to make the boat more comfortable for you.

Voila!

Synergy!

Now that sounds reasonable, that has substance and heft, don't you agree?

That's how to make a boat move! Think about *that* during your next race.

("Advice worth the price of this book and more in that one sentence yessirree, and if you act now we'll throw in the Popeil pocket stroke meter absolutely free. A $29.95 value. But you must act now. Operators standing by. Out of town call collect.")

Try this. When I was in a race, I used to ask myself, "How much harder can I pull? How much harder can I hit the catch?"

Completely wrong. No prizes for pulling hard.

None.

Tiff tells me that all he thinks about in a race is getting ahead and staying ahead. That's better. They *do* give prizes for getting ahead and staying there.

But take it a step further. Ask yourself, "How far can I send the boat on each stroke?" That's *how* you get ahead and stay ahead.

Now take the next logical step. Ask yourself, "How can I assist and enhance the efforts of my teammates to send the boat on each stroke?"

Do all this . . . and you will be reinventing yourself as a rower, and you will be amazed at the difference.

* * * * *

How good is this Tiff Wood? He won a bronze medal at the Worlds in the single in 1983.

That good.

My old friend Ted Van Dusen, remember he who relegated me to fourth in the 1972 dash while rowing in his homemade boat? Well, he kept on making boats, got pretty good at it (but I'll bet you already figured that out), and he made a very special boat with a sliding rigger that Tiff used at the Worlds in 1983.

220

Afterwards the boat was destined for the scrap heap, engineers like Ted being so darned unsentimental, so to save it I bought it from him, rowed it daily for a few years and then donated it to the National Rowing Foundation.

Today you can visit it at Mystic Seaport.

You can visit Ted in his shop outside Boston, Tiff in the suburbs of Portland, Oregon and Jim Dietz at UMass, where he's coaching.

Antiques all now, as am I, but Tiff tells me he is still rowing in masters events.

"Tiff, have you changed any? Has your approach to moving boats evolved over the last fifteen years?"

"I doubt it." So says Tiff Wood.

I love this man!

* * * * *

"Tiff, my good friend, my comrade in arms, I am sitting at my desk in my home in Del Mar, California, and I realize now that I have been writing this book just for you. If you, and no one else on this Earth, if you alone gain some additional insight into rowing by reading this book, then I will have achieved my goal."

New Casks

In Tiff Wood's day, Olympic Rowing Trials didn't get on television In this millennial year, as I write this book, apparently they do.

Not because the public gives any more of a rat's ass, but I suppos because cable TV needs something to put on all those channels.

And so I have gotten the opportunity to take a good, hard look a some of the best our country has to offer as this latest Olympi quadrennial comes to a head.

More old wine in new casks, I'm afraid.

Nothing much has changed since 1984. I wonder if any of this new generation has even read *The Amateurs*.

> *"Those who cannot remember the past*
> *are condemned to repeat it."*
> — George Santayana

As I watch the men's single final frame-by-frame I keep sayin, under my breath, "I sure could make *that* guy ten seconds faster!"

Here, at the dawn of the new century, the most famous and worth sportsman in the world is a polite young man named Tiger Woods.

A golfer! Not even an athlete like us! Instead, a player of games!

He was already the greatest golfer the world had ever seen in 1997 won the U.S. Masters Golf Tournament by a record twelve strokes.

Horizon job!

But he wasn't satisfied, not one bit.

He went to his coach and said he wanted to improve his game.

"What for?" his coach might have asked in 1997.

"What for?" you might also want to ask today. "What on God' Green Earth for?"

"Because," Tiger might reply, if he were here.

And so Tiger and his coach went about completely re-engineerin, his golf swing, back to basics, at great personal cost to Tiger Woods.

Changed his whole philosophy, and for more than a year Tiger struggled with the unfamiliarity. Didn't win a single tournament. People started whispering.

"Flash in the pan. Too bad. Probably seen the last of that nice boy, Tiger Woods."

Just the other day Tiger won the U.S. Open by fifteen strokes, another record. Wasn't it the same weekend as the Olympic Trials?

Too bad Tiger Woods doesn't row. With an attitude like his, "I sure could make *that* guy ten seconds faster!"

Now that fellow who won our Olympic Single's Trials? By his own admission in the post-race TV interview, he's already achieved a lifelong ambition, to represent his country in the single.

Between you and me, he needs some fundamental technique work. Back to basics, yessiree.

But would he have the courage to make the sacrifice Tiger Woods did? Now that he's already achieved his lifelong ambition?

Would he risk all he has and start over?

Or couldn't he much more easily rationalize that he's already the best in America. Isn't that enough?

And isn't it?

So what if he is destined to get his ass kicked in Sydney by athletes he could beat, oh yes he could *beat,* if he only rowed up to his potential?

So what? He'll do okay.

And does he even have the time in his life to start over? Our sport makes us give up a Hell of a lot in lifestyle and career if we want to follow our dreams past college.

By contrast, old Tiger probably had to scrape by on a few hundred thousand in winnings and only few million more in endorsements during his year in outer darkness.

"Just do it."
- Tiger Woods

Because

Hard to feel sorry for old Tiger Woods, economizing like that for whole year, but I *do* feel sorry for that guy who won the Singles Trials He's so big, so muscular, and he rows that way, drunk with power.

Better keep the Alka-Seltzer handy. He'll wake up with a hangove in Sydney.

The Trials-winning men's quad is also drunk with power as I watc them on TV. Whose videos could have they been studying? Stephen W Hawking? Joe Cocker? Katherine Hepburn?

Forget fundamentals. Not even a hint of stroke mechanics. O timing. Or even bladework.
Even bladework!
Our Olympic Team, for Heaven's sake.

Just a bunch of hackers.

Big, strong ones, to be sure! And oh-so-*worthy* of our admiration fo their dedication and for what they have accomplished, for they are trul our best and brightest, the best in America.
But forget about boat moving.
Forget about that last three or four percent of efficiency. Forge about aspiring to achieve their very best!
Just imagine what these fine athletes could accomplish if onl somebody told them that rowing is about style and technique and not *jus* about power!

Oh my!

But power is poisonous honey.

> *"Why row well when you can row hard?"*
> - 2000 U.S. Olympic Team

"Because," Tiger Woods might reply if he were here.

The Emperor's New Clothes

I'm sure a few of you are now thinking, "How *dare* you criticize our Olympic Team?"

I'm reminded of the Emperor's new clothes.

Is nobody allowed to cast a critical eye on our National Teams?

And why not?

It seems to me that, just as we get the Congress we deserve, the Congress we support with hard money and soft money, the Congress we demand special favors from, the Congress we vote for, we also get the Olympic Team we deserve.

They are a mirror in which we see our own reflections. If our Olympic Team has no appreciation for technique, it is only because the American rowing community has no appreciation for technique.

> *"We have met the enemy, and they are us!"*
> - Pogo

The two most thoughtful and sensitive people I have met in my entire life of rowing are Tom McKibbon and Frank Cunningham. I am pleased to report they are respected amongst rowers. I submit they *should* be revered. They are national treasures.

* * * * *

I have watched more than a few Olympic regattas in my time, and there has been a recurring pattern. At some point in an Olympic cycle, a coach who has had legitimate success at the World Championships is given a multiple-year mandate to produce an Olympic champion eight. More than once, as the years would go by, their eight would go slower and slower and finally fail miserably at the Olympics.

As you know, Allen Rosenberg pulled together a group of experienced veterans and won the World Championships in 1974.

Bravo!

He was then appointed National Coach through Montreal, two years later.

Here's his record:

1974 – first
1975 – fifth
1976 – ninth

I was there in Montreal, as you know, and it was so sad. Our beautiful 1974 eight had completely lost its swing, lost its run. They were rowing in concrete. They were killing fish!

How could this have happened? More than one observer has opined that the more of Allen's Sequential Style the guys absorbed over the years, the slower they went.

* * * * *

I was also there in 1996 to see the women's eight.

Oh . . . my . . . God!

They had been fast in 1994 and 1995. But it seems they spent the entire year before Atlanta pounding away, trying to become tougher and more aggressive than Romania, their main competition.

What was the result? Power is poisonous honey, even for women. Especially for women!

"I sure could make *that* boat fifteen seconds faster!"

They were *that* dreadful, the most disappointing performance by a U.S. Olympic boat in my lifetime. No run. No swing. Not even *close* to a medal.

I felt so sorry for them. It sure wasn't for lack of effort or dedication or talent or strength or fitness.

It wasn't the athletes' fault!!!

Watching them row reminded me of that tiger in *Little Black Sambo* who chased himself around a tree, faster and faster, trying harder and harder, expending more and more energy until he finally turned into a blur and churned himself into butter.

* * * * *

For those of you upset about my lack of political correctness in mentioning a book that I learned to read with fifty years ago, a book that happens to include a racial stereotype, I'll confess to you I also thought Buckwheat was funny on the *Little Rascals*, watched *Amos and Andy* and went to Bo Diddley concerts with the black woman who helped to raise me, and I go back to Indianapolis, Indiana to visit her every year.

I also marched for civil rights. My late mother was co-founder of the Indianapolis Urban League. I taught elementary school in North Philadelphia and worked in the Black Panther breakfast program.

I encourage you not to underestimate me.

* * * * *

Back to that terribly disappointing women's 1996 Olympic Eight. Didn't anybody figure out what was so tragically wrong?

Doesn't anybody on our Olympic staff understand that rowing is more than ergometer scores? that pounding away will only get you so far? that boat moving is crucial to real success in international rowing? that technique is crucial to real success in *life?*

I've been told a story about our own 2000 Women's Olympic Eight, now training for Sydney. Apparently the woman in the stroke seat can't hold a candle to her teammates on the ergometer or on the weights . . . but she kills everybody in singles and in seat racing, and nobody seems to have a clue as to why. Big mystery . . .
"Hello?"
Let me *give* you a clue. She surges to the end of her strokes!
She moves boats!

Isn't it time to teach the other seven women in the Olympic Eight to move boats, too?

Isn't it time to teach *the entire country* to move boats, too? No time like the present to start preparing for the 2004 games.

* * * * *

Incidentally, the gold medal for the women's eight at the Atlanta Olympics was won by a boatload of *small-boat* world champions from Romania, strong and tough as Hell, to be sure, but they had a sculler's touch. They surged. They had swing. And they kicked ass!

Are you paying attention?

Time Machine II

Let's revisit my own greatest triumph as a rower, far below the Olympic Trials as it might be, let's re-examine the 1966 Canadian Henley from the perspective of boat moving.

My perfect race in St. Catherines occurred when we were all relaxed, under no pressure, not trying too hard, and too tired to hit the catch.

Insight!

Subconsciously we were making up for not exploding at the catch, like we were supposed to do, by stroking to the finish of each stroke, which nobody ever asked us to do, except maybe in a single.

And we had been sculling all summer.

Hmm!

But power is poisonous honey, even at 145 pounds. It seduces and kills.

The very next day, when we were again besotted with our own muscular potential, again strong enough to row the way we had been taught, we were back to being mere mortals.

Hmm!

As I have already told you, God, I used to wish I had a time machine. What I would have given to spend just a few minutes with myself back then. Wouldn't have taken much to straighten me out!

"I sure could make THAT guy twenty seconds faster!"

It is stunning how a subtle change in approach, in attitude can make such a tremendous transformation in the performance of a boat.

Stunning!

Are you paying attention?

Who are you, Peter?

With no time machine forthcoming, by the late 80s I was ready t retire from coaching. My lifelong quest for the secret of boat movin had reached its end. And so in 1988 I poured all my efforts into one la boat, a San Diego Rowing Club junior quad . . .

And nobody noticed.

(No wonder I'm such a fatuous fussbudget, honey!)

That '88 boat was based on a junior lightweight cox four that wo the Nationals for me in 1987, relegating to a distant second a St. Joe' Prep crew that had won the U.S. Schoolboy Title for my old friend Bruc Konopka.

That four of mine included Mark Skirgaudas, a brooding blond wit a quick mouth and a thousand-mile stare, Lars Caroe, the best pure hig school athlete I had ever coached, and brothers Guymon and Br Casady, sons of my good friend and Masters pair partner, Kent Casady.

After we won in '87, Guymon graduated, went on to Penn an became a fellow Quaker, and so the following year we replaced him wit Mike McCormick. In addition, Jimmy Warmington would drive dow from his home in Newport Beach to join us on weekends, an rower/cox'n Kristin Bailey would steer whenever needed.

Now that I had the secret to boat moving, we aimed high. Our goa was to qualify for two U.S. World Championships teams.

A daunting task for five little boys!

I kid you not! Little boys.

Get this. We wanted to go to the Nations Cup Under-2 Championships in Hazewinkel, Belgium in the lightweight quad even but we were all under eighteen and so would give up four years o maturity to our competitors.

Eighteen to twenty-two. Four important years!

If that wasn't enough, we were so light we would also give up nearl five kilos per man to everyone else.

Eleven pounds!

230

If that wasn't enough, we also wanted to go to the Junior (under 18) World Championships two weeks later in Milan, Italy in the open quad event, where at least we were the right age, but since they had no lightweight events, we'd be giving up more than twenty kilos per man.

Forty-four pounds! More or less.

They were the more. We were the less.

Oh my!

I used every tool I knew to teach these guys to move boats: video, computers, endless long-distance practices in single wherries . . .

. . . and they were magnificent.

My best work ever.

* * * * *

Early in the spring of 1988 we need to test ourselves to be sure we are ready for the challenges ahead. Fortunately, the fastest junior eight in the country the previous year had been Marin Rowing Association. They are only 500 miles to the North of us, and they are all coming back!

I call up their crusty coach, Lou Lindsey, and tell him I want to race his best four guys in a cox four, his absolute best guys, and we will drive up to their boathouse to do it. We agree on a date, and then he asks me who we are.

"Who are you, Peter?

"Who *are* you?"

Good question!

He doesn't remember any studs from San Diego last year. I explain that we won the Nationals in the lightweight junior four in '87 and that we're training for the World Trials in a quad this year.

He says, "Fine, I'll send out my best lightweights."

I reply, "No, your best *heavyweights*, the stern four of your varsity eight!"

He says, "I can't do that. It would be too embarrassing for you."

We go back and forth. It takes several phone calls. Each time I insist, he reluctantly agrees . . . and then he says we can row his JV guys, and we start all over again three days later.

On the appointed day, when I pull into the Marin parking lot with the trailer I am actually looking forward to having to roll that rock up the hill one more time.

No need, it turns out. *Alle ist klar.*

The Marin course is on San Francisco Bay north of the Golden Gate Bridge and in the shadow of San Quentin Prison.

Talk about atmosphere!

We draw up to the starting line against two Marin cox fours, the bow and stern fours of their undefeated varsity eight.

And we lose . . . by just under a length over 1,500 meters. Their stern four averaging maybe 190 to our 145, and they just grind it out, stroke-by-stroke, inch-by-inch. It's a great race.

The bow four? A hundred meters back?

Something like that.

Then we jump into our quad and race them again in their eight. We lead off the line, but they steadily pull through. Win by just under ten seconds.

* * * * *

How good were these Marin guys? In the junior eight they win the Southwest U.S. Regionals by over twelve seconds. We had petitioned to enter the event ourselves with our quad, but the word was out that we had come closer to Marin than anybody else had during the entire season, and so we are excluded by a vote of the other coaches.

Wise move. Chickencrap, but wise.

No urban legend experience for us. Too bad. Then maybe somebody might have noticed.

In the heavyweight junior cox four? Marin beats us again at the Regionals, again by just under a length, our two boats twenty seconds or more ahead of everybody else.

Oh yes. Then the Marin stern four goes on to the National Team Selection Camp . . . and becomes the stern four of the National Junior Eight that goes to the Junior Worlds in Milan.

Bravo Lou Lindsay! Bravo Marin Rowing Association!

And bravo San Diego!

At the Southwest Regionals along with our silver behind Marin in the heavyweight junior four we win golds in the heavyweight junior single, double and quad and the lightweight junior four.

Then we win the heavyweight junior quad at the U.S. Nationals by eighteen seconds . . .

. . . one, one thousand, two, one thousand . . .

. . . and then we qualify to represent the United States of America at both World Championships.

So there!

With five boys. My five little boys.

* * * * *

How did we do in Europe? Sad to say, here's where you start dismissing me.

We didn't actually beat *anybody*. Last at the Nations Cup, but less than a length behind Portugal's National Composite Squad, our tiny team of five little boys from a single club in California against their tiny country.

But a *country*, for Heaven's sake! With a government and a federation and a language and a history and a culture and a fishing industry and an opposition party and a tourist office and an embassy in Washington.

A country. Yes, Portugal is a *real* country.

We were also last at the Junior Worlds, but this time less than a length behind Great Britain.

Our tiny team again. Our five boys. Bigger country, this time. Bigger embassy in Washington. Better television. Always liked *Masterpiece Theatre*.

Then, the boys all graduated.   Two went to Yale, one each to Stanford, UCLA and Orange Coast.

My best work.

photo credit: Peter Mallory

1988 Texaco/San Diego Rowing Club/USA
U.S. Junior Quad Champions
Two-Time U.S. Trials winners:
Junior Heavyweight Quad, Under-22 Lightweight Quad
Stroke Bret Casady, Mark Skirgaudas, Jimmy Warmington, Lars Caroe.

Could you match that pounding the catch?
Before you dismiss me, you give it a try.

For His Taste

Interesting follow-up story about Mark Skirgaudas, one of the two fellows who went on to Yale. The next year he rowed six seat in their first freshman lightweight boat, but his coach, Andy Card, never particularly liked the way he rowed. Didn't hit the catch quite hard enough for his taste. Accused him of sculling.

How many times must we hear this crap?

Now this Andy Card is no lightweight, at least not figuratively speaking. As an athlete, he was an E.A.R.C. champion and a Henley champion at Princeton. He would soon coach the 1993 World Champion U.S. Lightweight Straight Four and the 1999 World Champion U.S. Lightweight Eight, not to mention a boatload of Eastern Sprint and national collegiate champion Yale crews. Doesn't sound like his taste for explosive power has exactly been holding him back or anything.
No way he was going to listen to little freshman Mark Skirgaudas back in 1989.

Or me, either, today in 2000, I'd venture to guess.

But, I confess, it would mean a lot to me if he did, this man I have never met.
Even *I* respect Andy Card's accomplishments more than I do mine.

Anyway, after freshman year Mark moved up to the varsity squad. Fortunately for Yale, unfortunately for Mark, so did Andy.

Their disagreement lasted three more years.

Now Mark would be the first to admit that he's not always the easiest guy to get along with, and, truth be told, he didn't make much of an effort with Andy.
After all, Mark never respected Andy's judgment all that much.

You see, Mark never lost a single seat race in all his days at Yale. Not a one.

And nobody noticed.

How many times must we hear this crap?

Mark never did get to see the inside of a Yale varsity lightweight eight on race day, which, to Andy's credit, was undefeated sophomore year despite Mark's exclusion . . .

. . . and so Mark Skirgaudas had to console himself with going to Henley his senior year as a member of a magnificent undefeated Yale JV, a swinging, surging boat that was a pleasure to row in, a boat Andy ignored until almost the end of the season.

After all, they didn't seem to hit the catch quite hard enough for his taste.

Incidentally, Andy's varsity wasn't good enough to go to Henley. Not that year, anyway.

Seriously. How many times must we hear this crap?

The Full Set

After 1988 I retired from coaching and dedicated the next year of my life to putting into practice all that I had learned, into competing as an athlete one last time, to willing the JV Scar to finally heal.

* * * * *

And so here I am rowing the semifinals at the Master's Nationals in the company of good friends who know how to move boats. And I have helped each one of them gain that insight.

But this isn't the first time I have surrounded myself with the fruits of my labors.

* * * * *

At the 1975 San Diego Crew Classic, I rowed in a lightweight four with Rod Johnson, from my 1974 LBRA Trials four, who would become a world silver medalist in the U.S. eight that very year, with John Fletcher, from my undefeated 1974 Cal State Long Beach lightweight eight and my 1974 Trials four, who would become a world silver medalist in the eight in 1977, and with young Scotty Roop, who had moved to Long Beach from Buffalo West Side a year too late to row for me, and who would go on to become a world bronze medalist in the eight in 1976 and then a world gold medalist in the lightweight single in 1981 . . .
. . . oh yes, and then Scott would go on to coach a national champion varsity crew at Brown University. (As I sit here today, he's at Henley with his crew.)

So, in our four, we had the full set: gold, silver, bronze and me!

We won the Crew Classic that day in 1975, and I bask in the reflected glory of my teammates and the small contribution I made to their lives.

What made that particular win additionally satisfying was the fa
that we had to beat a fine four from San Diego State, who pressed us a
the way down the course.

photo credit: the Mallory Collection

1975 San Diego Crew Classic Champion Lightweight Four
Cox'n Jeanne Bedford, stroke Rod Johnson, Peter Mallory,
Scotty Roop, bow John Fletcher.

I did it all again at the 1976 Crew Classic, teamed up with three ne
mates, Tom Bowman and Steve Estes, both on my coaching staff a
Mission Bay, and Bob Miller, a Naval officer stationed in town.

Again our competition came from San Diego State. Again we wo
but it was oh-so-close.

Afterward, every one of the State guys became tremendous friends.

Perry Alexander graduated and became a minister. Perhaps bein
around the rest of us convinced him the world needed a great deal of hel
. . . and who could disagree about *that!*

Phil Arcidiacono achieved additional success rowing for me an
made it all the way to the final cut at the National Team Selection Camp.

Hunter Minnix is still rowing, still winking at life, still competin
today.

238

And not only is Chris Anderson still rowing, he has won multiple, multiple National Masters Championships and even served as president of San Diego Rowing Club.

And, twenty-five years later, he still makes weight!

I am honored to have twice crossed the line ahead of these fine athletes.

It's the competitors that make the race. No point in winning if you don't respect the crews you beat.

A Bunch of High School Kids

Halfway down the course in Oakland, my mind snaps back to the race at hand.

It occurs to me that for twenty-three years (and now it's thirty-four years, I can report in retrospect) John Cantrill, 155 pounds in Canada back in 1966, has been accusing me and the other Undine 145s of having beaten up on a bunch of high school kids during our perfect race in St. Catherines.

"They weren't ALL from high school . . . were they, John?"

Well, where's the phone? I need to call John right now! All these crews at the 1989 Master's Nationals certainly aren't high school kids.

Big field. Twenty-plus boats in the field. Biggest in the regatta. Biggest ever, in fact. For the Audi Cup.

"We're kicking ass, John. If you weren't impressed in 1966, be impressed today, John.

"We know how to move boats now . . . every time. We have trained for it, and now we are in command of our semi-final."

And, best yet, I remind myself, our good friends from TRW Rowing Club are cutting a similar swath through the other half of the field.

I can't wait for the final.

Time Flies

E.A.R.C.   Eastern Area Rowing Colleges.   E.A.R.C. Sprint
Championships. What's been my lifetime record?

My freshman year I end up as the Penn first boat spare.   Got to
watch my teammates tie Cornell for second place.
Tie Cornell! Can you believe that? Pretty good. Very good!

And Columbia was *first!*
No seriously.   Columbia.   Their first freshmen were terrific that
particular year.
What's the expression?

"Sometimes it even snows in Del Mar, California."
- Del Mar Chamber of Commerce

(It must be snowing today.   As I write this book, the Columbia
Lightweights are competing at Henley.
The Royal Henley.
What do you bet Norman Hildesheim is over there covering them for
the *New York Times*?)

Back to the E.A.R.C..
We were twelfth and last my sophomore year.   (Columbia kicked our
Quaker asses, all of you Baby Blue alums will be overjoyed to hear.)
Only one victory for us that year.   We actually beat Rutgers during
the season, and that was cause for quite a celebration.   Beating Rutgers
on their home course on the Raritan River in New Brunswick, New
Jersey, had been the first win by the Penn Lightweight Varsity in at least
three seasons, ouch . . . and the first win by *any* Penn boat in almost a
year, *double ouch!*
(Remember, I picked Penn because they had a crappy lightweight
crew, and, boy, did I get what I wished for!)
. . . but then at the Eastern Sprints, the E.A.R.C., Rutgers rebounded
and rowed through us at the 800-meter mark of the petite final.
At the end?   DFL.   That was us.   Same for our lightweight freshmen
and JVs.
After only one year under Fred Leonard, we still barely had a pulse!

But then the climb began.
Fifth junior year.
Then second (in the JV) my senior year.

Then three more seconds as a freshman coach.

You know, in my whole career I only got to participate in a single
E.A.R.C. victory . . . and that at one degree of separation.

In 1976, three years after I left the East Coast, I got a phone call a
couple of hours after the E.A.R.C. lightweight varsity final.   Mark
Davison and his mates from my 1973 freshmen crew, the guys who
began their E.A.R.C. careers in the line squall, were drunk with victory
. . and drunk with alcohol as well, truth be told. They had tracked me
down in California to tell me they had won the Sprints, the first Penn
Lightweight Varsity to do so since 1955, when I was ten years old and
before most of them were even born, and now they were going to
Henley. They remembered me, were grateful to me.
    And I was grateful to them.
    They cried. I cried.

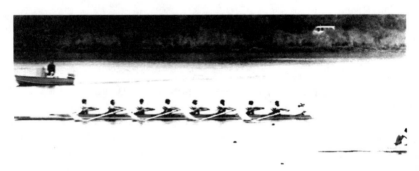

photo credit: Sam Lamar

1976 Penn Lightweights beating Harvard to win the Eastern Sprints.

I got to row in their boat at their tenth reunion.   1986.   They were
terrific. My best early work as a coach. I basked in their reflected glory.
Still do.

242

Twenty-fifth anniversary next year. Sam Lamar won't be there. He's already in Heaven, was in a Hell of a hurry to get there, too. Been there quite some time now, I'm sad to say.

"Say hi to Galen, Sam, and put in a good word for us. We'll all be with you soon enough."

Time flies, you know.

Catty Wampus

By 1989, I have come to assume the E.A.R.C. is far behind me. I'm a Californian, for Heaven's sake . . . and an old man.

Lot of water under the bridge, over the dam.

Then early this summer of 1989 I finally run into Eric Loberg.

. . . Cornell, Class of 1967.

. . . E.A.R.C. Varsity Lightweight Champion.

. . . the guy Chris Williams tried to introduce to me twenty-two years earlier, the guy who wanted to take exception to the Harrison/Mallory sign: "Lightweight Rowing's Strongest Weight Lifting Pair."

Is this a small world or what?

Eric Loberg's an orthodontist now, puts braces on kids' teeth, and he's rowing for TRW in Los Angeles!

We meet them and beat them handily at the Long Beach Invitational,

photo credit: the Van Dillen Collection

San Diego Rowing Club (background) winning handily in Long Beach, TRW (foreground) in second, everybody else WB (way back).

but it's quite a bit closer by Marina del Rey.

And no wonder.

Another Cornell lightweight is in their four, Billy Brown, class of '69.

Is this a small world or what?

244

Another Pickwickian coincidence! Yessirree! The very same Billy Brown who had been my Cornell JV counterpart in 1967, who had won my shirt by one foot in the Penn-Cornell dual meet, but who had been relegated, *by me*, to third place in the E.A.R.C. Sprints, and on the very last stroke! Oh yes!

I remember it like it was *yesterday!*

TRW even sports a third E.A.R.C. rower, Dave Van Dillen, Rutgers 1967, a Scarlet Knight, but a heavyweight this time, so we never actually met on the water back in our salad days. Sweet man now. Probably was sweet back then, too.

Old Home Week in Oakland. U.S.R.A. Nationals. E.A.R.C. reunion.

photo credit: the Van Dillen Collection

1989 TRW Rowing Club Masters B Cox Four
Carbo Loading
Eric Loberg, Billy Brown, Eric Atkins, Dave Van Dillen
Helen Wong

Had I the gift of foresight back in 1989, I might have asked Eric Loberg, "Eric, what do you know about the Rutgers guy, Dave Van

Dillen, just in case eleven years from now I decide to go out and write a book about our upcoming race for the national championship?

"Just in case . . . "

And, back then, Eric's reply might well have been, "I don't know. He's the only one of us who actually works for TRW. He's a civil engineer, so he doesn't talk much.

"We train in a pair together against the other two guys. That's how we got fast.

"Oh, Helen Wong, our cox'n, she works for TRW, too.

"I don't know . . . That's it.

"And what's this about a book?"

The TRW Crew is completed by Eric Atkins, a UCLA heavyweight.

And so I might have continued my inquiry, "How about the UCLA guy?"

"What's to know? He went to UCLA. Other than that, he just sits in the boat and rows hard.

"What else do you have to know about a person?"

I *love* this man!

You know, a lot of people might conclude that's all there is to Eric Loberg, just a single-minded, ambitious, middle-aged jock.

I'll tell you a secret. He's a big softie.

He's the man who inspired me to write this book, and you know how he did it? At the 2000 San Diego Crew Classic, we stopped and talked. My son, Philip, was with me. Well, Eric Loberg, D.M.D., took one look at Philip's teeth and wouldn't let go of me until I promised to take him to an orthodontist immediately. Gave me a bunch of referrals.

At that moment I decided I had to write this book and spill the beans on Eric Loberg, tell everyone what a kind and caring person Eric Loberg really is. The big softie!

But don't let on you know. It'll be our secret.

Let's let Eric continue, as only Eric can.

Remember how I told you my freshman year Penn tied Cornell for second at the Sprints . . . and Columbia was first? Here's Eric Loberg's take on the race:

"Tied us? Tied us? I'll *tell* you how you guys tied us.

"We were all ready to beat those Columbia bastards, but we crabbed at the 800 meter mark . . . and I should know because *I was the son of a bitch who caught the crab!"*

In response I can only say, "General Patton, *sir,* yes *sir!"*

I love this man!

* * * * *

Funny thing. The world has gone catty wampus in two decades. In the old days, my Penn boats would hammer away at 35 or so, while Cornell would settle to a 29 or 30 and just *crush* us with pure, old-fashioned boat moving.
But TRW . . .
The concepts of ratio and slide control are extinct, dead as a dodo. Why, they row like the Cambrian Explosion, primitive and brutal.

Sound familiar?

"Technique is for *wimps!"* Eric is fond of saying these days, Eric who rows like he drinks beer.

"Keep 'em coming, bartender."
- Eric Loberg, D.M.D.

Now *we* are the boat movers, the technicians, and the Cornellians are the hammers. Full circle.
I'm getting a headache!

But it is more than that, more than rowing. TRW does everything with such *gusto!*

I can't wait to see these TRW guys at every regatta. Big smiles. Bigger handshakes. We've stayed ahead of them all summer, but they aren't holding it against us. This is true brotherhood of sport. I never looked forward so much to racing my guts out as I have this summer.

And what a rich history we have between us! More than twenty years!

You may recall that while I was kicking Billy Brown's ass at the Sprints in 1967, Eric Loberg was relegating the Penn Varsity to second while I watched, rubbing my thigh.

Then Eric and Chris Williams and the rest of that superb Cornell first boat went on to Henley.

* * * * *

Interesting place.
Henley-on-Thames, England.

The river's rather narrow that far upstream of London, only two boats across, or so I'm told, never having been there myself. Seen a lot of pictures, of course. The start of the course, a mile and five-sixteenths upstream (But you knew that!), is amongst open fields with just a smattering of onlookers.

As Cornell lines up the first day, their cox'n calls over to their opponents, suggesting the two crews bet shirts on the outcome, just like we do in the States.

From the shoreline:

"My God, Maude, the colonists wish to wager the sweaters off their backs!"

Maude swoons.

"I salute you, Eric Loberg." You have done something I always wanted to do.

* * * * *

And now we cross paths again.

Billy, too. "How's Alfalfa? How's Darla?"

Now your boat and mine, we are lined up at the starting line of the rowing course on lovely Lake Merritt in downtown Oakland, California, birthplace of the Black Panther Party.

Oakland, a big-shouldered city with docks Jack London used to haunt, a city down the street from the Berkeley campus, home of Nobel laureates, the Whole Earth Catalogue and the Free Speech Movement. Oakland, within the kill zone of the Lawrence Livermore Laboratories, across San Francisco Bay from Alcatraz and Ghirardelli Chocolates.

Half a lifetime . . . and half a world and more away from Henley-on-Thames.

Far even from Lake Quinsigamond, ancestral home of the E.A.R.C.

"What a long, strange trip it's been."
                    - the Grateful Dead

The U.S. National Finals.

Six boats. But actually there are only two real boats we care about, only two boats with any chance at all in this race this day.

"Captain Eric, this is Captain Tim and Captain Glenn. Captain Dave, this is Captain Tim and Captain Glenn. Captain Tim, . . . "

My boat and yours. San Diego and TRW? No, one last time it's Penn and Cornell.

It's personal.

"Cornell, Cornell, B.M.A."
"Hurrah . . . Hurrah . . . Hurrah . . . Hurrah . . ."

E.A.R.C. reunion indeed!

Foma

It's a funny thing, this . . . thing . . . this national championship, half a lifetime in the making.

All the disappointments, all the dreams, ever unfulfilled . . .

. . . this national championship . . .

In his sad and frustrating book, Harvard Crew dropout Craig Lambert put the quest for greatness this way: "Valleys of discouragement and doubt interpose themselves between desire and fulfillment, between wanting a gold medal and wearing one."

" . . . between wanting a gold medal and wearing one." A little heavy on the *foma*, to be sure, but still I like that last phrase.

"I sure could make *that* guy forty-five seconds faster!"

(That's not fatuous, honey. He seems like a sincere guy, and he really deserves better advice than he's gotten!)

"You are *still* being sold a bill of goods, Craig!

"Call me! I'm in the phone book!"

But now the Nationals are over, our Nationals, my Nationals, and there's been a Doppler Effect.

> " . . . *ding,ding,ding,ding,*
>
> *dong,dong,dong,dong* . . . "
> - *Pet Sounds*, the Beach Boys

Something you looked forward to with such anticipation and trepidation for ***twenty-five years*** . . .

. . . suddenly changes pitch . . . now seems so matter-of-fact, so routine, so . . . inevitable when you look back on it from a perspective of ***twenty-five minutes.***

Of course, I have become a national champion.

OF COURSE!

I was completely prepared. All my rubber ducks in a row. (Excuse the pun.) I had been around the world and back to build this boat.

Paid my dues.

The rigging was prefect. I've contributed that. We had trained ourselves to the very limits of our imaginations. Glenn gets the credit there. We were the most disciplined, right Rick? We were the biggest. The strongest. The fittest.

And we were the prettiest, too. That was Tim's department.

Yes, we were the best.

The best in the country.

All of it on a foundation a quarter-century in the building, brick by brick. Thanks in no small part to my lifelong quest, we knew how to move boats. We rowed better than anybody.

Than everybody!

Wasn't this what I've made my journey for? Isn't this the end of the rainbow?

The Grail?

The Fleece?

I've hung in there, oh yes I had! All those disappointments, those long years and countless miles since my first trip to the Nationals in 1965. . .

. . . since my first out-of-boat experience!

Now we are national champions. I wear the fact like a comfortable flannel shirt on a wintry night, snow glistening in the moonlight through the window, me sitting in front of a cozy, crackling fire, my wife cuddling at my side.

Now it all seems so inescapable, so predestined, so normal even. I suppose when you climb Mount Everest, the last few steps seem an anticlimax.

A journey of a thousand miles . . . ends with a walk in the park.

* * * * *

After the award ceremony, with the sun shining on my gold medal, John Biglen rowing across its surface, on *my* gold medal hanging around *my* neck, the sun shining on the Audi Cup cradled in *my* arms, I run into Eric Loberg behind the Lake Merritt Boathouse.

He's pretty disappointed.

I've grabbed his gusto, stunk his spunk.

In all the twenty-two years since Henley he had not picked up an oar. Then, just a few months ago, he ran into Billy Brown at an Our Gang reunion, and that was that. In a burst of anatomical mixed metaphor, he turned his back on running 10k's on old knees and returned to our beloved sit-down sport as if he'd never left it.

With a vengeance!

This was the first year TRW had come to the Nationals to race the world, to race SDRC, to race Tim and Glenn in a four. They discovered we were close to perennial champions back then.

We *owned* the B four back then!

Eric refers to Tim and Glenn, my esteemed stern pair, as "those upside down triangles rowing in front of you." Apparently, I am equally impressed. After all, I put them on the cover of this book!

But now TRW had Eric, and Eric was not used to losing, could probably count his losses on one hand, by golly . . .

. . . and this was the first year someone as "ordinary" as I had been included in San Diego's signature boat.

Hell, I only got the seat because Dennis Whelan, a large to my medium, was skipping the regatta to go to his twentieth high school reunion.

And I was bald and gray. I was *old!* Quite a bit older than my teammates, as old as the TRW guys, one foot practically in the grave, for Heaven's sake! I had been coach and mentor to my teammates, to all of them, for Heaven's sake!

A father figure of sorts, with all the good and bad connotations that follow.

This had to be TRW's best chance. *Had* to be! If they didn't beat San Diego with an old Penn lightweight, an old Penn *JV* lightweight in the boat, then they never would.

(Never did, I can report with hindsight.)

252

Could Have Rattled a "Crew Team"

And the race had been sooooo close. For them, defeat snatched from the jaws of victory. It really hurts to be rowed down from behind as the finish line approaches.

(Or so I'm told. Never happened to me. Ever. Mighty proud of that statistic.)

For TRW Rowing Club of Los Angeles, California, had led us off the line. First time all year we had been behind anybody.

The couple of times we had already raced TRW before Oakland, sure they'd been in the neighborhood, sure we respected them, but each time we had won, and each time we had taken them off the line. No one could keep up with us at the start.

No one!

And so our race plan for the national final had been simple:

1. Do our jobs.
2. Collect our gold medals.

Take the lead, as always, with our patented twenty-stroke start, then cruise another 300 meters or so to the 500-meter mark, and then begin our gradual build to finish.

Just like in practice. Do our jobs.

Êtes vous prêt? Partez!

By twenty strokes we are two seats down.
Down! *Down!* As in behind. Not first. Out of the lead.
And two seats is a *lot* in twenty strokes! Nothing to sneeze at.
This is *not* part of our race plan!

And they're moving away!

Big surprise. Caught *my* attention! Yessirree! Could have rattled a less experienced crew.
Could have rattled a "crew team."

So we get maybe five strokes past our racing start, and Kristin says coldness in her voice: "We can't wait 'til the 500, guys. We have to g now."

Now?

"Have you lost your mind? Are you trying to suggest that we jus finished our start, and we have to begin our sprint . . . already?"

Could have rattled a crew team.

I remember our training: the endless steady state, the 250s, 500s 750s, repeat, repeat, repeat, repeat. The weights. The running. The squat leaps. The ergs.

I'm ready.

We just go. Tim changes the rhythm subtly, and we just go.
We're swinging. VroooOOOOOOM!
Every stroke.

Magnificent! God-like . . .

Staunch the Wound

Kristin shades her eyes and gives us the bad news. They're *still* moving.

photo credit: the Loberg Collection

SDRC cox'n Kristin Bailey shades her eyes and gives us the bad news.

It takes a full twenty strokes, twenty magnificent strokes, the best twenty we can give, to stem the tide, staunch the wound.
Finally we are holding them.

Nevertheless, we find ourselves more than four seats down with less than 500 meters to go in our 1,000-meter race.
Four seats.
No time to wonder what our chances might be. No time to contemplate whether I will ever again in my lifetime be granted such a golden opportunity.

No time for one last out-of-boat experience in my life, no time for such self-indulgence, but still I think . . .

I've come a long way. 1965, '66, '67, '68, '69, '71, '72, then all the coaching, all in a blur. Lot at stake here. Lot of people counting on me. Even beyond my teammates in this four.

Always tried to be an inspiration, a role model to more that a thousand people over the years by now.

Now they perch on my shoulders.

There is ever more purpose in Tim's rowing. He has come a long way, too. UCI, SDSU, MBRA, Penn A.C., the Pan Am's, SDRC, always fighting a bad back.

And Glenn. He invited me to row in this boat three months ago. Brought a tear to both our eyes. Come a long way together.

And Rick. Did every workout all year by himself on his ergometer in his apartment in Atlanta between Delta flights.

Can you believe that?

No rowing clubs in South Georgia. Phoned in his results to San Diego.

Talk about iron will . . .

"My hat's off to you, sir."

Yes! Now we are edging back.

But not by much.

Will there be time? What are they thinking? Over there?

God, they must be flying!

A hundred meters ago, did they assume they had us beat?

I did.

"Hurrah . . . Hurrah . . . Hurrah . . . Hurrah . . ."

We have some momentum now, but still it will be close.

Twenty-five strokes or so to go, by my count. Not a lot of time left but my oar is fueled with confidence and pride and destiny.

In the Gut

Ten strokes to go. There *must* have been a moment when we were dead even, but I missed it. We have surged past them, our stroke continuing to climb. Won't even be close now at the end.

And then it is over.

. . . three feet? A meter after 1,000 meters?
. . . three feet. A heartbeat. A hiccup.

Doppler
        Effect.

No euphoria.
Friendship. Gratitude. Honor. Relief.
Family. Team is Family.

Validation!

> *"Hokey Smokes, Bullwinkle!"*
>   -   Rocket J. Squirrel

* * * * *

And now I am behind the boathouse, and Eric Loberg is poking me in the gut. With his pointy finger.

Hard for you to imagine you have been beaten by someone with a gut hanging out, even a little? Your chest is as big as mine. Bigger. How do you hold your gut in so well? If I weren't so embarrassed, I'd ask you what your secret is.

Sit-ups? I'd done a ton of sit-ups. Can't be sit-ups. I'd made a religion of sit-ups.

How could you look so good? I swear. You must wear a goddam girdle!

Getting old is Hell! Did you know a few years later I would get liposuction in an effort to lose that gut of mine, all because of you and your pointy finger?

257

You still poke me in the gut. Every time you see me. It's okay. I deserve it.

It's your right, my friend.

1989 TRW Rowing Club Masters B Cox Four
Bow Billy Brown, Eric Loberg, Eric Atkins, stroke Dave Van Dillen
Cox'n Helen Wong
National Silver, Personal Gold

Anyway, Eric, when I ran into you that afternoon, I told you that you deserved the gold medal as much as me. Our two boats, we had elevated ourselves to a plane above all the others. The few feet between our bow balls at the finish line hardly seemed as relevant as the reality that all eight of us, all ten of us, had done extraordinary things to get to that finish line, done things over the course of years, of decades, that all of us belong to the same elite fraternity.

The same family.

We are brothers and sisters.

Eric, did I convince you that you put the luster on my gold medal? Here's what you said to me:

"You guys did a great job! . . . and you got the *best* from us!"

Worth training a year for . . . just to hear that.

258

Worth training a lifetime for, in fact.
Worth writing a book about, don't you think?

Thank you, my good friend.

Now you got *me* sounding like a big softie.

* * * * *

Did you know the next day I won another national championship, in a quad this time, by only a few inches this time, certainly less than a foot, and on the very last stroke this time, in the company of other equally good friends this time, and cared not nearly the same this time, for I did not respect the competition, nameless and faceless to me, as I had respected Billy Brown, Eric Loberg, Eric Atkins, Dave Van Dillen, and Helen Wong?

So it goes.

* * * * *

Our four? I finally got a photo of my national champion boat, a magnificent photo taken at the start by those nice people at *SportGraphics*, got it framed with the medal, hung it on the wall, just like I planned so many years ago.

I still have it. Just ask me. I'll be happy to show it to you.

Epilogue

And so I left Lake Merritt having come full circle, having completed a sentimental journey and returned to my metaphorical Ithaca to vanquish the suitors, the mighty Cornellians, after a twenty-two-year journey.

I returned to my Penelope, my wife Susan, fat and pregnant with our unplanned second child, a girl we had decided to name Katherine Jean, Jean after Susan's mother, Katherine after my Aunt Kate.

Never really considered Zulette . . .

Two years earlier Susan had won the Master's A Single Sculls event at the Nationals in Lake Placid. Never seen a shell before she met me, never seen a scull, either, but she learned well. Hell of a competitor. Knew how to move boats. I taught her.

And courageous?

The nine months had come and gone, and the birth pains had begun before I even left home for Oakland, before the National Regatta had even commenced!

Katie's coming! *Êtes vous prêt?*

The very day before I left, my boss, Don Lang, hosted a late summer gathering on his sailboat. When, in the course of polite conversation, I mentioned I was about to leave for three days to go to the Nationals, Don's wife Karen did a double take, took another look at Susan's enormous abdomen and asked when the baby was due.

"Yesterday . . . tomorrow . . . any second, basically," replied Susan nonchalantly.

Karen turned to me.

"And you're leaving? To go *row?*"

Before I could even open my mouth Susan retorted, but oh-so-politely.

"A child takes only nine months, Karen. As a family we committed to the Nationals way before we committed to this baby."

Only a rower could say those words. And Susan was a *rower!* Yessirree!

260

Thank you, Susan.

Karen Lang, definitely *not* a rower and always one to speak her mind, looked me straight in the eye and said, "I always knew you were an asshole, Peter. This just confirms it."

At that moment, I can tell you I prayed she wasn't right.
At least not that time.

And I realized it had been a very long time since I got a kick out of hearing an adult cuss me out.

But when I returned home four days later, still our daughter remained content in the womb.
Truly the stuff of myth, worthy of Homer, don't you think?

Katie was born the day after I returned from the Nationals. I was present for the event, weak-kneed and much relieved.

Another decade and more has now gone by. Don has divorced Karen. Susan has divorced me. We all say, "Good riddance! Hurrah!"
How sad.

But I continue to pour my energy into my family . . .
. . . into my new wife Jeni, sweet Jeni, who doesn't row, thank Heavens, who doesn't think I'm an asshole, at least not any more than I deserve, thank Heavens.

> *"And now a quarter of my life has almost passed.*
> [I *wish* it was only a quarter!]
> *I think I've come to see myself at last,*
> *And I see that the time spent confused*
> *Was the time that I spent without you."*
> — John Sebastian

. . . into my Tellemachus, my son Philip Rogers Mallory II, named after his great-grandfather, who rowed at Yale, ran Mystic Seaport and spent a lifetime close to the water, among his many other accomplishments.

Zut alors! He's studying French in honor of his grandfather, who grew up on the Continent and rowed at Kent and Yale, among his many other accomplishments.

And now he rows himself and is occasionally coached by me, his father, who rowed at Kamp Kill Kare and Kent and Penn and Undine and Cannotaggio Firenze and Vesper and Harvard and Cambridge and Long Beach and Princeton and ZLAC and MBRA and Club Nautilus Klagenfurt and SDRC and now has even written a book about it, among my other meager accomplishments.

Philip wears my old rowing shirts, my Penn letter sweater. He has calluses on his hands and stories of his own to tell now.

And so the circle begins again.

But Philip is way ahead of me. He already knows the secret . . . my gift, my legacy to him . . . Even at an impatient 97 pounds (!) he knows how to move boats . . . He rows like God!

"Someday, Philip, people will finally notice you, appreciate you. I promise."

photo credit: SportGraphics

2000 San Diego Rowing Club B Entry, Novice Junior Quad With
Southwest U.S. Regional Bronze Medalists
Cox'n Megan McQuown (barely visible), bow Tom Beban (Zaphod Beeblebrox),
Tom Shook, Tom Considine, stroke Philip Mallory

Don't see my Katie as much any more. Lives with her mother these days.

My loss.

But every time we talk about her birth on April 22, 1989, she reminds me:

"I waited for you, Daddy."
- Katherine Jean Mallory

Absolutely true story. *Couldn't* make any of this stuff up.

I can rest now. I'm having an out-of-book experience.

Order Form

AN OUT-OF-BOAT EXPERIENCE

. . . or

God is a Rower and He Rows Like *Me!*
by Peter Mallory
One *very* opinionated man's journey in the sport of rowing.

NAME _____

ADDRESS _____

CITY _____

STATE _____ ZIP _____

Yes, please send the following books:

_____ copies of

AN OUT-OF-BOAT EXPERIENCE
@ $18.95 per copy $_____
Postage & Handling ($4.00 per book)   _____
In CA, add 7.75% ($1.47 per book)   _____
Total (cashier's check or money order) $_____

(Quantity discounts available upon request:
         team_mallory@hotmail.com or FAX (619) 224-0530)

Mail to:
San Diego Writers' Monthly Press
3910 Chapman Street
San Diego, CA 92110-5694